FUN

ANIMAL FACTS

AND TRIVIA

FOR KIDS

CHUKU MICHAEL

Table of Contents

Introduction

Imagine your child hanging out with friends, and someone brings up a topic about animals. Suddenly, your child gets stuck, not knowing what to say or saying something incorrect or boring. This situation can greatly damage the confidence of any child and this is one of the reasons I wrote this book.

This book isn't just about fun facts. It's a treasure chest of knowledge designed to make sure your child is never caught off guard again.

As a parent, this book is your secret weapon for keeping your child engaged, entertained, and informed. It's packed with fascinating trivia that not only captures a child's curiosity but also enhances their knowledge in ways that will benefit them both at school and in social settings.

Think about the benefits of knowing awesome facts like **how tigers' saliva acts like an antiseptic, helping them clean wounds, or how lions eat wild lemons when they're thirsty and can't find water.** Now imagine your child confidently sharing these facts, impressing their friends and teachers. Facts like this doesn't just fill a kid's mind with cool information; it sharpens their ability to remember, communicate, and think critically.

Research shows that reading fact-based books can help children develop cognitive skills, increase their ability to recall information, and even improve their critical thinking abilities. According to a study published by the **National Literacy Trust**, children who read nonfiction books, such as trivia or fact books, are more likely to develop problem-solving skills and are often more engaged learners. Engaging with these kinds of books can foster a love for learning, curiosity, and imagination, leading to lifelong benefits in school and beyond.

What's even more fun is that kids can read this book anywhere! Whether they're in the car on a long road trip, curled up in bed before sleep, or enjoying some quiet time at school, the amazing world of animals will keep them captivated. From learning about **swifts that can fly for six months without landing, to wood frogs that can freeze themselves for seven months**, every page is filled with jaw-dropping facts that make learning feel like an adventure.

This book will not only entertain your child but also boost their confidence in conversations, spark new interests, and even reduce screen time in a way that feels like play, not work. And with mind-blowing details like how ostriches can kick hard enough to kill a lion or how horses can sleep standing up because of a special leg-locking system, your child will always have something interesting to share.

Dive into "Animal Facts and Trivia for Kids" and discover how knowledge can be both fun and empowering!

.

DOWNLOAD 50 FREE WORD SEARCH PUZZLES FOR KIDS

Please Visit: funsided.com/puzzle

OR

- Open your camera app or QR code Scanner.

- Point your mobile device at the QR code below

- The download page will appear in your web browser.

Tiger Facts

1. The stripes that each tiger has are different from that of another tiger, just like the human fingerprints.

2. Tigers can mimic the sounds of other animals to lure them to their death.

3. When a tiger urinates, the pee smells like popcorn that is buttered.

4. The type of animals that a tiger eats depends on its territory and it can eat up to 75 lbs (34kg) at once.

5. Interestingly, for two weeks on a stretch, a tiger can go on without feeding.

6. Because they are hunted for their skin and meat, tigers are in the category of highly endangered animals.

7. The reason why tigers eat human beings is that they feel threatened by the way humans behave.

8. When a mother tiger gives birth, the cubs are normally 3 in number, but they can give birth to up to 6 cubs at once.

9. The number of days that it takes for the newly born cubs to open their eyes is 10 to 14 days.

10. The rate at which tiger cubs die in childhood is high, only about one tiger cub out of three live up to adulthood.

11. Tiger cubs stay with their mothers for about 2 and a half years before they start fending for themselves.

12. Tigers love water and are both good hunters and swimmers.

13. The saliva of a tiger has antiseptic qualities and they make use of it to clean up their wounds to avoid infection.

14. Although only for short distances, a tiger can run up to 60km per hour (37.28 mph).

15. A punch from a tiger is so strong that it can break a human bone or lead to instant death.

16. Whenever a tiger feels that its territory is safe, it closes its eyes in contentment.

17. One of the notable things is that they sleep a lot, tigers can sleep up to 18 hours each day.

18. The number of people that tiger has killed is bigger than that of lion and leopard combined.

19. The eyes of a tiger can see very well at the night, it is 6 times better than a human's eye.

20. The taste buds of tigers are created in a way that they cannot detect sweetness.

21. When a tiger dies, the hind legs are so powerful that they can still support the tiger to stand even after death.

Lion Facts

1. You can determine how old a lion is by checking how dark the mane is, the darker the mane, the older they are.

2. The chance of a male lion surviving to adulthood is slim, with about 1 in 8 making it to adulthood.

3. Lions have the weakest bite when compared with other big cats at 600 psi.

4. Lions spend most of their day sleeping, they can sleep up to 21 hours daily.

5. When a kill is made, the alpha male lets the female have 90% of the share.

6. Lions scavenge more than 60% of their daily food.

7. The tongue of a lion is created in a special way; it is rough enough to peel away the flesh from the back of human skin.

8. A lion cannot roar until they grow up to the age of 2 year.

3

9. A lion has a black spot that is at the base of its whisker that is just as unique as human fingerprints.

10. The lion's ear is so enhanced that it can hear the sound of prey about a mile away.

11. A pregnant lioness hides to give birth and hides the lion cub(s) for six weeks before bringing them to the pride.

12. When there is a scarcity of water, lions eat wild lemon to keep hydrated.

13. Since lions also derive fluids from their prey, they can go for 5 days without drinking water.

14. Unlike some other big cats, lions do not chew their food before swallowing.

15. The heels of a lion do not touch or reach the ground while moving.

16. Male lions protect their territory, which can be as large as 100 square miles, by marking it with their scent and patrolling the area.

17. Lions communicate through a series of roars, grunts, moans, and growls, each having a different meaning.

18. Female lions synchronize births so cubs can grow up together and be raised collectively by the pride.

19. Lions have retractable claws, allowing them to keep them sharp for hunting and climbing.

20. A lion's heart is about the size of a human fist, proportionately smaller compared to other big cats, meaning they rely on stealth and strategy rather than endurance during hunts.

21. Despite their dominance, lions only succeed in about 30% of hunts, which means survival is often a challenge.

Leopard Facts

1. Just like tigers, the spots of a leopard are unique from other leopard like human fingerprints.

2. The gestation period of a leopard is very short, it carries its pregnancy for about 96 days before giving birth.

3. Leopards know how to climb a tree very well and they store what they kill on top of a tree.

4. When a leopard is roaring, it sounds like a chainsaw cutting through a tough tree trunk.

5. Leopards can live without drinking water for as long as 10 days.

6. Leopards can jump very well and can leap 6 meters (20 feet) into the air.

7. Leopards come together to breed.

8. Leopards are able to roar just like lions but are rarely heard doing so.

9. Leopards are the most widely distributed African big cat.

10. Their coat color and rosette patterns are dependent on their location.

11. Black leopards exist but are rarely seen.

12. Leopards can see seven times better in the dark than humans.

13. They can move heavy carcasses 3 times heavier than them up a tree.

14. The largest prey reportedly killed by a leopard was a 900 kilograms male eland.

15. Leopards can eat anything from dung beetles to savannah and plains antelope.

16. There are nine subspecies of leopards and are distinguished by their coats.

17. Leopards are characterized by relatively short legs and a long body with a large skull.

18. Male leopards weigh from 37-90 kilograms and females 28-60 kilograms.

19. Leopards can adapt to various habitats ranging from rainforest to steppe.

20. The size of a leopard depends on its geographical location.

Cheetah Facts

1. The cheetah is not able to roar like other big cats.

2. 10% of the kills that a cheetah makes are abandoned to other bigger cats like lions.

3. The spots that a cheetah has are just as distinctive as human fingerprints.

4. Cheetahs can go for 4 days without water since their environment doesn't have much water around.

5. Unlike all the other big cats, cheetahs are able to turn mid-air when they are chasing prey.

6. The mortality rate of cheetah cubs is very high, 95% of its children don't make it to adulthood.

7. Cheetah cubs are introduced to meat when they are three weeks old.

8. Unlike other big cats, cheetahs don't have good night vision for hunting.

9. Cheetahs have what act like sunglasses that protect their eyes from the sun as they hunt.

10. Cheetahs are not able to climb trees like leopards or tigers because of their non-retractable claws.

11. When they are faced with a hyena, Cheetahs prefer to stay away.

12. The cheetah can have between 2,000 and 3,000 spots.

13. Female adult cheetahs often live alone and only meet with the males to breed.

14. Cheetahs can anticipate the escape tactics of different prey when hunting.

15. Cheetah's diet consists of impalas, wildebeest calves, gazelles, and other smaller hoofed animals.

16. The body of a cheetah is characterized by a slender body with long legs.

17. Depending on the species, Cheetahs can weigh from 46 – 159 pounds and 112 – 150 cm in height.

Jaguars Facts

1. In America, the biggest cat is not a lion or a tiger, but jaguars.

2. Jaguars have a layer of fat under their skin that helps them maintain body temperature, especially in colder regions.

3. The shape of spots that are on the jaguar's skin is shaped like a rose.

4. The geographical location of a jaguar is what determines its size.

5. The markings on a jaguar's skin have distinctive features like human fingerprints.

6. In the wild, jaguars can live up to 12 years, while those in captivity can live up to 20 years or more.

7. Unlike many other big cats, jaguars are excellent swimmers and often hunt in water, preying on fish, caimans, and even anacondas.

8. Among other big cats, jaguars have the strongest jaw.

9. Jaguars are nearly as fast as a cheetah, running up to 80 km per hour.

10. The cubs of a jaguar are born blind and they are only able to see after two weeks after birth.

11. When a jaguar cub is born, the eyes are blue, but they turn yellow to red as they grow.

12. The tongue of a jaguar is rough enough to lick off flesh from its prey's body.

13. When a jaguar cub is born, it is born deaf and will regain hearing after a few weeks.

14. Naturally, jaguars run away whenever they perceive that a human is coming.

15. Jaguars are solitary animals (animals that do not live together) and only come together to mate.

16. Jaguar habitat ranges from southern England to Nebraska and down into South America.

17. Jaguar is characterized by their stocky build with short, powerful legs.

18. Males normally weigh between 56 to 96 kg and the smallest females weigh about 36 kg.

19. A female jaguar typically gives birth to 2 to 4 cubs after a gestation period of about 93 to 105 days.

20. The tracks of jaguars can be distinguished from those of other big cats by their large, round shape, often appearing as a single track rather than a paw print with distinct toes.

Cougar Facts

1. Unlike most big cats in the wild, the sense of smell of cougars is not sharp.

2. Cougars are highly endangered animals, with only about 334 remaining on earth.

3. Cougars are impressive jumpers and can jump up to 20 feet (6.1 meters) into the air.

4. Only the female cougar is involved in taking care of the cougar cubs.

5. Cougar cubs are born with blue eyes and it usually takes 18 months for them to transform to the normal cougar eye color.

6. The location at which a cougar is staying is what determines its size and weight.

7. Unlike most big cats like lions and tigers, cougars are not able to roar.

8. Cougars hold a record in the Guinness Book of Records as the animal with the greatest number of names, with over 40 in English alone.

9. Unlike what many people believe, there is nothing like a black cougar.

10. Cougars usually hunt one large mammal once every two weeks.

11. There are about six subspecies of cougars and they all have different sizes.

12. Cougars have a bad sense of smell but make it up with a good sight.

13. Cougars are good swimmers but they prefer not to go into the water.

14. Male cougars can weigh up to 200 pounds (90.7kg), while females only weigh up to 120 pounds (54.4kg).

15. No animal species prey upon fully grown cougars in the wild except humans.

16. On average, cougars grow to between 5 (1.52 m) and 9 feet (2.74 m).

17. Cougars are the most widely distributed land mammal in the Western Hemisphere.

50 General Animal Facts

1. The loudest animal on earth is not the elephant, but the blue whale.

2. The only specie of bird on earth that is able to fly backwards is the hummingbird.

3. Despite what we see, flamingos are not meant to be pink, but get the color because of a natural pink dye called canthaxanthin contained in their diet.

4. The deadliest animal on earth isn't the lion nor is it a snake, but the mosquito which kills more than 700,000 people per year.

5. The most deadly snake on earth is the Inland Taipan, whose venom can kill 100 people.

6. In order not to float away from each other while sleeping, otters hold hands with each other.

7. The animal that has the shortest lifespan is the Mayfly they live for about 24 hours.

8. Koalas sleep a lot and can spend 22 hours each day sleeping.

9. The crowing of roosters has the same sound energy as a running chainsaw.

10. Pangolins roll up into an armor-plated ball to prevent predators from eating them.

Image of Pangolins

11. Swifts fly a lot and can fly for an entire six months without landing.

12. Blue whales are very big and their tongues can weigh up to a car or approximately 2.7 tons.

13. Dying at the age of 189, the longest living verified land animal is Seychelles giant tortoise.

14. The animal that is the fastest in the sea is the sailfish which can swim up to 68 mph (109 kph).

15. The fastest bird on earth is the peregrine falcon which can dive at the speed of 242 mph(389 kph).

16. Just as babies suck on their thumbs, elephant babies suck on their trunks to find comfort.

17. The strongest bite of all animals on earth is that of the Salt water crocodile, which can apply over 5,000 pounds (2267.96kg) of pressure per sq inch.

18. The male seahorse, pipefish, and sea dragons are the only male animal that naturally gives birth to their younger ones rather than the females.

An Image of a Puffer fish

19. The puffer fish contains a toxin that is able to kill 30 people and it has no verified antidote.

20. The land animal that has the loudest noise is the howler monkey which produces sounds that can be heard 5km away.

21. The eyes of the colossal squids are as large as a basketball and they can see 400ft away.

22. In every acre of green land, there are approximately 50,000 spiders around.

23. The gray-headed albatross fly a lot and can circle the whole earth in about 46 days.

24. The legs of an ostrich are so strong that they can kill a lion with a kick.

25. Half of all the pigs on earth had their home in China, with about 440 million pigs.

26. Hippos secrete a natural sunscreen, called "blood sweat," which is red and protects them from UV rays and infections. Polar Bears are only white on their furs but have black skin under them.

27. The Giant anteater eats a lot of ants and can consume about 35,000 ants in 24 hours.

28. The Great White Shark can detect a drop of blood from a far distance, about 5km (3.1 miles) away.

29. For up to 18 minutes, a Naked Mole Rat can be able to survive in a zero oxygen condition.

30. The irritating spray of the skunk is able to cause temporary blindness in its victims.

31. The most venomous fish is not the jellyfish, but the 30cm Stonefish whose sting is extremely painful.

Image of a Jellyfish

32. The horns of a rhinoceros are made of the same material as human hair and fingernails.

Image of a rhinoceros

33. When food availability is low, the edible dormouse is able to hibernate for about 11 months.

34. The biggest insect that was recorded was the dragonfly which had a wingspan of about 2 and a half feet.

35. The Greenland sharks live the longest and one of them is said to be over 400 years old.

36. The fastest movement that was recorded in the animal kingdom is that of the Dracula ant that snaps its mandible.

37. The toxins of a box jellyfish are strong enough to kill someone before they are taken to the shore.

38. Some female albatrosses prefer to bond with their fellow gender.

39. Corvids, which include ravens, crows, and rooks, are extremely intelligent and can understand how gravity works.

40. Tardigrades known as water bears have the ability to survive for ten years without food. It is important to point out that it is a microscopic organism.

41. Sheep are able to recognize people that are familiar with them.

42. The only species of bird that have the ruminant digestive system is the Hoatzin.

43. The Yangtze giant soft shell turtle has a weight of between 150 to 220 kg and is the largest freshwater turtle.

44. The Mariana sailfish has its home 8000 meters deep into the ocean, which makes it the deepest fish in the ocean.

45. The basilisk lizard can run on water, earning it the nickname "Jesus lizard."

An Image of a basilisk lizard

46. The lungfish is the only fish in the world that has both gills and lungs in its body system.

47. The electric shocks that electric eels give are strong enough to make a horse faint.

48. The Patu Digua is a spider so small that the head of a pin is 4 times bigger than it.

49. The male yellow head jawfish stores all the eggs in his mouth for it to hatch.

Image of yellow head Jawfish

50. The heart of a blue whale is so large that a human could crawl through its arteries.

Facts about Bees

1. The only insect on earth that produces what human beings eat is the bees.

2. A bee is capable of flying all over the world once it has an ounce of honey as food.

3. Unlike what people think, the bees are quite fast, reaching up to 15 miles per hour (24km/h).

4. The honey that the bees produce is a combination of 20% water and 80% sugar.

5. The queen bee lives for 2 to 3 years on earth.

6. The queen bee does a lot of work; she lays about 1500 eggs each day.

7. The worker bee has the shortest lifespan in the colony, with only four weeks to live.

8. The bee wax that bees produce comes from an eight-paired gland that is under their abdomen.

9. During the late spring and early summer, as many as 50,000 bees stay inside the colony.

10. It takes a lot of bees to produce one teaspoon of honey as one honey bee produces only 1/12th of the honey on the teaspoon.

11. The reason why bees make a buzzing sound is that they stroke their wings about 11,400 times every minute.

12. The honey that bees produce can stay for many years without spoiling, up to a century.

13. For a nectar collection trip, a bee has to visit an average of 50 to 100 flowers.

14. Bees perform a "waggle dance" to communicate the direction and distance of food sources to other members of the hive.

15. Archaeologists have discovered pots of honey in ancient Egyptian tombs that are over 3,000 years old and still perfectly edible.

16. Research shows that bees can recognize and remember human faces by associating facial features with patterns, much like we do.

17. The queen bee is fed a special substance called royal jelly, which allows her to live up to five years, much longer than worker bees.

18. Honey bees can regulate the temperature of their hive by clustering together and vibrating their wing muscles to generate heat or by fanning their wings to cool the hive down.

19. Bees are responsible for pollinating about 75% of the world's flowering plants, including around 35% of the crops that feed humans.

Frog Facts

1. The frog lives almost everywhere in the world except for Antarctica.

2. The frog makes use of its bright coloration for warning and camouflage.

3. The eye position of the frog is unique, with a 180 degrees view.

4. Unlike many animals, frogs have to close their eyes before they can eat.

5. Although most frogs live beside the water, they don't drink water, it absorbs them with their skin.

6. Most frogs are poisonous and the most poisonous of them all is the Golden Poison Frog.

7. Frogs have been on earth for a long time, more than 200 million years.

8. The largest frog in the world is larger than a newborn baby and weighs 7 pounds (3.2kg).

9. While some frogs are very big, some are very small, and the smallest is only 0.27 inches (0.69cm) long.

10. Just what they are known for, frogs jump a lot and some of them can jump 60 times their body length.

11. Some frogs that live in the desert can hibernate for up to 7 years as they wait for rain.

12. The upper jaws of the frog act as the teeth, to hold their prey before they swallow.

13. Snakes sometimes steal the venom of a frog by feeding on them.

14. The size of a frog depends on the species and geographical location.

Turtle Facts

1. Large sharks are the common predators of sea turtles.

2. Turtles can sleep up to 5 hours underwater.

3. Turtles are cold-blooded because they are reptiles.

4. Soft-shell turtles have flattened shells but they are carnivorous and aggressive hunters.

5. Jonathan the tortoise, is the oldest living tortoise on land at approximately 189 years old,
6. The leatherback turtle is the biggest and largest species of turtle.

7. Turtles don't have teeth, rather they have beaks like birds for breaking down food.

8. Bigger turtles live longer than the smaller ones and can live up to or more than 100 years.

9. Turtles can't live without their shells, unlike what people believe.

10. Some species of turtles are known to weigh more than 300 kilograms or 661 lbs.

11. The giant tortoise is among the biggest species of tortoise in the world.

12. The rear flippers of sea turtles are used as rudders to steer in the water.

13. Snapping turtles are heavier than the usual species of turtles.

14. The inner shell of turtles has about 60 bones including the ribs and the backbone.

15. There are so many turtles that there are over 350 species of turtles in the world.

16. Most species of turtles are able to live both on land and in water.

Horse Facts

1. The skeleton of a horse is made up of about two hundred and five bones.

2. Because of a special locking system in their legs, horses can sleep while standing and lying down.

3. Horses have bigger eyes than any other land mammal on earth.

4. The teeth of a horse take up more space in their heads than their brains.

5. Horses are not able to vomit because they have a strong band of muscles around their esophagus.

6. Horses salivate a lot and can produce approximately 10 gallons (37.85 liters) of saliva a day.

7. The tallest horse on record was the Shire named Sampson which was 7 feet 2 inches (2.2 m) tall.

8. According to studies, there are approximately sixty million horses in the world.

9. Horses don't have a collarbone, rather a sling of muscles and ligaments connects their skeleton to the rest of their body.

10. The brain of a horse weighs about half of the human brain at 623 grams.

11. Horses drink a lot and drink at least five gallons of water each day.

12. The heart of a horse is like the size of a basketball and typically weighs between 4kg and 4.5kg.

13. The only outlet horses can breathe in the air is through their nose and not their mouth.

14. Horses have ten ear muscles, while human beings have three.

15. The world's smallest horse breed is the Falabella which ranges from 38-76 cm tall.

16. It is illegal to open or close an umbrella in the presence of a horse in New York City.

Squirrel Facts

1. Squirrels are able to live up to ten to twenty years in captivity and five to ten years in the wild.

2. Although squirrels are herbivores, they are able to eat insects and butterflies.

3. Squirrels are not that heavy and weigh between 12 to 26 grams.

4. The oldest squirrel fossil that was found was about 11.6 million years old.

5. Squirrel bites and scratches are able to transmit dangerous diseases.

6. Not all squirrels hibernate during the winter such as the tree squirrels.

7. The breeding time of squirrels is different depending on the species.

8. Depending on the species, female squirrels can have more than 10 babies at a time.

9. Interestingly, baby squirrels have their eyes closed and are pink in color when they are born.

10. Female squirrels' pregnancy lasts for about twenty-five to forty-five days.

11. 25% of a squirrel's food cache gets stolen by other squirrels or other animals.

12. The biggest squirrels in the whole world are the giant black squirrel species.

13. When squirrels wag their tails, they are not happy, they are upset.

14. To make sure that they survive, squirrels must gather and bury as much food as they can before winter.

15. Squirrels are so cooperative that they will warn other squirrels if they see something suspicious or dangerous.

16. A squirrel's tooth is irreplaceable once it has fallen out.

Dog Facts

1. Dogs are capable of understanding up to 250 words and gestures, performing complex tasks, and even solving puzzles.

2. Dogs have as many as 300 million receptors compared to humans 5 million.

3. Seventy percent of people in the world sign their dog's name on their holiday cards.

4. Unlike what people think, The Basenji is not technically "barkless," they can yodel.

5. A dog's tail is not just for balance—it's a communication tool. The direction and height of their tail wag can indicate different emotions like happiness, nervousness, or alertness.

6. 46% of United States dogs sleep in the bed of their owners.

7. A dog's nose print is unique and can be compared to a human's fingerprint.

8. The Bloodhound's sense of smell is so accurate that the findings of its tracking may be used as evidence in court.

9. Dalmatians are born completely white and develop their spots as they get older.

10. The Norwegian Lundehund is the least popular dog breed among all the dog breeds in the world.

11. Unlike what people think, Labrador Retrievers are originally from Newfoundland.

12. The Australian Shepherd is an American breed and not from Australia.

13. A Mastiff named Zorba is the world's overall largest dog ever at 343 pounds(155.6kg).

14. Greyhounds can beat cheetahs in a long-distance race as they can keep up with their 35 mph (56kph) speed for 5 miles (8km).

15. The only breed of dog named for a fictional person is Dandie Dinmont Terrier.

16. There are over 340 different dog breeds worldwide, with each having unique traits, temperaments, and purposes.

17. Dogs can sense natural disasters like earthquakes before they happen, possibly because of their acute hearing and ability to detect subtle vibrations.

Cat facts

1. The peripheral vision and night vision of a cat are superior compared to humans.

2. Cats don't whisper only on their face, they also have a set of whiskers on the back of their front legs.

3. Cats sleep a lot and usually sleep around an average of 15 hours per day.

4. The wealthiest cat in the world is named Blackie and has a fortune of £7 million.

5. Cats have a whopping 32 muscles in each of their ears compared to human beings' 3 ear muscles.

6. Cats are impressive jumpers and can jump as high as five times their own height.

7. Cat whiskers perform a very important job and function in assisting cats with getting around, especially at night.

8. Surprisingly, house cats share 95.6 percent of their genetic makeup with tigers.

9. A female cat is able to become pregnant as early as 4 - 6 months of age.

10. Cats can beat the famous Usain Bolt in a 200-meter race as they can run to the speed of about 30 mph (48.2kph) over short distances.

11. In the past in Egypt, members of a family would shave their eyebrows if their cat died to mourn the cat.

12. The oldest cat ever lived for 38 years and 3 days old and was named Creme Puff.

13. Cats have 26 teeth when they are babies and they have 30 permanent teeth as adults.

14. If cats are able to put their rear end in your face, it means that they trust you.

15. Cats can have a dominant front paw, males tend to have a dominant left paw, while females have a right dominant   paw.

Elephant Facts

1. The two main species of elephants are the African elephant and the Asian elephant.

2. An elephant herd is headed by a female and not a male, and so is matriarchal.

3. 4% of African elephants are born without having a tusk.

4. Despite their huge bodies, elephants don't eat meat, they are vegetarians.

5. Ivory poaching is the main thing that makes elephants to be endangered, it involves killing elephants for their tusks.

6. Elephants Can Communicate Via Vibrations that are known as rumbles.

7. With an estimated 257,000,000,000 neurons in their whole nervous systems, elephants are very intelligent.

8. The skin of an elephant is very thick, the average elephant's skin can be around 2.5 cm thick all over its body.

9. Elephants eat a lot every day and Can Eat Up to 300pounds (136kg) of Food Every Day.

10. Because they are easy targets for predators, the average baby elephant can stand within 20 minutes of birth.

11. Every African elephant has a tusk, but Only Some Male Asian Elephants Have Tusks.

12. The body of an elephant is filled with a lot of muscles, and only their trunks alone have up to 4000 muscle units.

13. Elephants Have "Fingers" on Their Trunk for holding objects, African elephants have two while Asian elephants have one.

14. With an average height of 8 to 13 feet tall, Some African elephants can grow up to almost a story tall.

15. Elephants are very heavy, and for comparison, they can weigh the same way as a car or two.

Panda Facts

1. There are two species of pandas, the red panda, and the giant panda.

2. Red pandas have the ability to digest over 40 different species of bamboo and they prefer short to tall bamboo.

3. Although Red pandas eat plants a lot, they have the digestive anatomy of a carnivore.

4. One fascinating fact about red pandas is that they have a pseudo-thumb.

5. Red pandas prefer to eat leaf tips and shoots of the bamboo plant.

6. When Red pandas are born, they weigh anywhere from 3 to 4 ounces at birth.

7. It is hard for red pandas in the wild, as the mortality rate is high in their wild habitats.

8. In terms of life expectancy, a giant panda's year is equal to a human's three years.

9. Although they eat a lot of bamboos, their ability to digest bamboo is low at less than 20 percent.

10. The world's oldest giant panda, Xinxing, was aged 38 years and four months.

11. Giant pandas have a sixth finger that acts like a thumb.

12. Because of the too much bamboo they feed on every day, it can poop 28 kilograms of bamboo each day.

13. Giant pandas have this strange habit of abandoning a child if she has twins.

14. Giant pandas are good tree climbers and can start climbing expertly as early as 7 months old.

15. Pandas eat a lot of bamboos and spend as long as 12 hours eating 12 to 38 kg of bamboo.

16. Pandas are not able to hibernate because of their bamboo-based diet.

Bear Facts

1. The sun bear is the smallest of the bear species and it was falsely thought to be medicinal.

2. Only 1 bear species lives in the Southern Hemisphere and it is known as the spectacled bear.

3. Polar bears are marine animals and depend on the ocean for food.

4. Unlike what people think, black bears are not always black, as some of them are cinnamon-colored.

5. The most widespread bear species in the world is the brown bear.

6. Sloth bears make use of their lips like a vacuum to scup ants and termites.

7. The Polish Army in WW2 had a bear that carried shells to the frontline and was taught to salute.

8. Because they are invading each other's habitats, grizzlies and polar bears have children together and are called pizzlies.

9. 500g of polar bear liver contains about nine million international units of Vitamin A and can kill humans if ingested.

10. A grizzly bear's bite is so strong that it is able to crush a bowling ball.

11. There are some bears in Russia that have become addicted to sniffing Jet Fuel out of discarded barrels.

12. In Canada, residents sometimes leave their cars open to help someone escape in case there is a bear attack.

13. There are some black bears that are born white and are known as Spirit Bears.

14. Bears are pretty fast while running and can outrun the average human being.

15. A container needs to survive a 60-minute mauling by a grizzly bear to be certified as "bear-resistant".

16. The only place where you can find Kodiak bears is in the Kodiak Archipelago in Alaska.

Zebra Facts

1. There are three main species of zebra and they include the plains zebra, the Imperial Zebra, and the mountain zebra.

2. When faced with predators, zebras encircle an injured family member to protect it.

3. Zebras are impressive climbers and can climb up mountainsides in search of food.

4. Zebras don't have any particular territory, as they are constantly moving, looking for fresh green grass.

5. Zebras have excellent hearing that is far more improved than other animals.

6. Something that is not widely known is that underneath zebra's white coats is black skin.

7. Zebras can drink water once every five days without dying or getting sick.

8. Zebras are impressive runners and can run up to 40 miles per hour (64km/h).

9. The largest species of zebra is the Grevy's zebras, while the shortest species is the plains zebra.

10. Just like horses or donkeys, zebras usually sleep standing up.

11. Because of predators, six minutes after being born, zebra fouls are able to stand.

12. The most widespread species of zebra is the plains zebra.

13. Just like the human fingerprint, each zebra has a unique stripe pattern.

14. Zebras have excellent eyesight and are one of the few mammals that can see in color.

15. Zebras run in a zigzag pattern to prevent predators from catching up with them.

Insect Facts

1. Ladybirds avoid being killed by predators by playing dead.

2. Grasshoppers have been on earth for so long and existed before dinosaurs.

3. A sea skater's leg hair traps air, which helps them to float on water.

4. Butterflies taste the plants they want to lay their eggs on with their feet.

5. Some male stoneflies attract their female counterparts by doing push-ups.

6. Bulldog ants can jump so much that they can leap seven times the length of their bodies.

7. Mosquitoes are more attracted to smelly feet, so keep your feet clean always.

8. There are about 36 species of dragonfly found in the United Kingdom.

9. An ant-eating assassin bug scares its predators away by piling its victims onto its body.

10. Grasshoppers have special organs that store energy which they use for jumping.

11. Caterpillars have a lot of eyes which can be up to twelve eyes.

12. A single honey bee colony can produce around 220 jars of honey each year.

13. Dragonflies have been on earth for so long, up to 300 million years.

14. The stag beetle is the biggest species of insect to be found in the United Kingdom.

15. A ladybird eats a lot of ants and can eat more than 5,000 insects in its lifetime.

16. Fruit flies were the first living creatures on earth that were sent into space.

17. There are times when large groups of fireflies flash in unison.

18. Ants are incredibly strong for their size, capable of lifting objects 50 times heavier than themselves.

19. Termites work 24 hours a day, constantly chewing through wood and other materials without taking a break to rest.

20. Certain insects, like grasshoppers and crickets, can regrow lost legs over time.

Sloth Facts

1. When they're in captivity, sloths sleep a lot and can sleep up to 10 to 16 hours.

2. Sloths are native to Central and South America.

3. The lifespan of sloths is quite long, at about 25 to 30 years old.

4. Depending on the species, sloths can weigh from 2.2 kilograms to 10 kilograms.

5. The size of the population of sloths is very low and they are endangered at 500 to 1500 population count.

6. Sloths can swim about 3 to 4 times faster than their pace on land.

7. The head of a sloth is so flexible that it can turn to almost 270 degrees.

8. The digestion of food in a sloth's body is so slow that it takes 30 days for sloths to digest a leaf.

9. Sloths spend a lot of time hanging on trees, about 90% of their life.

10. When Sloths are inside the water they can hold their breath for 40 minutes straight.

11. Sloths have their organs attached to a rib cage which enables them to hang upside down.

12. Sloths' claws are so strong that they can grip trees even after death.

13. The tail of a sloth is so small that it has a length of around 3-5 cm only.

14. Baby sloths can live without their mother 6-11 months after birth.

15. About one-third of a sloth's body weight drops after it poops.

16. A sloth always has a smiling face whether it is depressed or angry.

Fox Facts

1. A study by scientists shows that foxes have domesticated themselves.

2. Bat-eared foxes make use of their 5 inches (12.7cm) ears to listen for insects to eat.

3. Foxes are so fast that they can run up to 42 miles per hour (67.6km/h).

4. The arctic foxes can survive harsh weather that doesn't shiver until -94°F.

5. The smallest fox weighs less than 3 pounds (1.4kg) and is known as the Fennec fox

6. Fox pup play can get violent and one out of five pups doesn't make it out of the den.

7. Fox pups become independent of their parents when they are 7 months old.

8. Fox pups are born helpless and blind until nine days after birth.

9. Foxes are one of the few animals on earth that make use of the earth's magnetic field. They utilize it to evaluate the distance between themselves and their prey, allowing them to perform a more precise pounce.

10. The most common species of fox in the world is the red fox.

11. Foxes have vertically oriented pupils that help them to see in dim light.

12. Foxes are solitary animals and prefer to stay alone rather than in groups.

13. Foxes are members of the Canidae family and are related to dogs.

14. Foxes live in every part of the world except Antarctica.

15. Foxes are usually most active after the sun goes down.

Kangaroo Facts

1. Male kangaroos impress their females by flexing their biceps (a muscle on the front part of the upper arm).

2. Kangaroos barely emit any methane and this helps to reduce greenhouse gasses.

3. Apart from Australia, France is another country that has a small population of kangaroos.

4. The possibility of hitting a kangaroo in Australia is so high that drivers fix metals in front of their cars to reduce the impact.

5. The meat of a kangaroo has a low-fat percentage that it has a 1-2 percent fat content.

6. Kangaroos are able to produce two different types of milk at the same time, for their new horns and young ones.

7. Female kangaroos have the ability to pause their pregnancies in times of drought or famine.

8. Kangaroos don't sweat and they keep cool by rubbing their saliva on their body.

9. Kangaroos are impressive jumpers and can jump 6 feet in one leap.

10. Kangaroos do kill a lot of people in Australia and more people are killed by kangaroos than sharks.

11. Kangaroos are one of the few animals that can't move backward.

12. Kangaroos are left-handed and the majority of their activities are done with their left hand.

13. Kangaroos are impressive runners and can reach speeds of over 35 miles per hour (56km/h).

14. Kangaroos retreat to bodies of water when they are being chased by predators.

15. Kangaroos know how to use a chokehold when there is a fight between them.

16. Kangaroos can't move their legs independently and this is why they hop.

Penguin Facts

1. Not all penguins live in the Antarctic such as the Galápagos penguin.

2. Penguins love staying in the water and spend up to 80% of their lives out at sea.

3. Penguins are waterproof and this is because of a spread of oil produced by the preen gland.

4. Emperor penguins have a weird habit of incubating their eggs with their feet.

5. Some penguin species stay with each other for the rest of their life.

6. Penguins don't have teeth; rather they have fleshy spines which they use to eat.

7. Gentoos are the speediest penguin species and can go up to 20 mph (32.2kph) in water.

8. The first name explorers gave penguins was "strange geese."

9. Penguins are impressive divers and can dive down over 800 feet into the water.

10. Emperor penguins are so big that they can grow up to four feet.

11. The smallest species of penguins is the Little Blue Penguin which doesn't weigh more than 3 pounds (1.4kg).

12. Penguins are native animals of the Southern Hemisphere.

13. Penguins jump into the air so that they can swim faster in the water.

14. The estimates of penguin species usually fall in the range of 17 to 20.

15. Generally, penguins swim at speeds over 10 miles per hour(16km/h).

Hippopotamus Facts

1. Hippopotamus are very dangerous to human beings and kill more than 430 people every year.

2. Hippopotamus likes to stay in the water and spend an average of 15 hours a day in the water.

3. A hippopotamus's average lifespan ranges from 40 to 50 years.

4. Hippopotamus prefers to give birth underwater because it is the safest place to do so.

5. Because they don't have furs around their body, hippopotamus secretes some natural chemicals to protect their bare skin from the tropical sun.

6. The hippopotamus eats a lot and can eat about 40 kilograms of food each day.

7. A hippopotamus's territory can stretch up to more than 200 meters.

8. Hippopotamus are very heavy and an adult male hippo weighs between 1500 to 1800 kilograms.

9. The bite of a hippopotamus is so strong that its force is up to 2,000 pounds per square inch.

10. A hippopotamus is capable of opening its mouth to full 150 degrees.

11. A group of the hippopotamus is called a herd or school and is made up of 7 to 35 hippopotamus.

12. Hippopotamus are very fast on land and can run at a speed of 30 kilometers per hour.

13. The hippopotamus is characterized by a barrel-shaped body, short legs, and long muzzles.

14. Hippopotamus are not so fast on water but can reach speeds of 8 kilometers per hour.

15. Hippopotamus has strong sets of teeth that are only used for fighting and not eating.

Spider Facts

1. The hair on a spider's first pair of legs is sensitive to taste and they make use of it to taste.

2. Most spiders eat their old web before starting a new one and they build new webs every day.

3. The average life of a spider is one to two years although some can live up to 20 years.

4. Spiders don't usually eat their prey, they put chemicals into their prey to turn the body into a liquid.

5. You are always three feet away from a spider because they are almost everywhere.

6. Most spiders are not dangerous to humans, especially the bigger ones.

7. The silk strands in a web are five times stronger than steel that is of the same size.

8. Spiders have short hair on their feet and this allows them to walk upside down.

9. There are so many spiders around that the average house has 30 spiders.

10. A spider takes about 60 minutes to spin a web every day.

11. Unlike what people think, spiders are not insects but are known as arachnids.

12. Except for the Arctic and Antarctic regions, spiders are found everywhere in the world.

13. The Wolf spider is one of the few species of spiders that carry their babies on their back.

14. Rafts spiders don't live on land like others, rather they live in water.

15. There are some spiders such as tarantulas that are kept as pets.

Lizard Facts

1. There are some species of lizards that can differentiate between colors.

2. There are some lizard species that can run backward with great speed.

3. Some species of lizards have a good vision that they can see ultraviolet (invisible light) light.

4. Gecko lizards are the species of lizards that are better than other lizards when it comes to climbing.

5. The tongues of some lizards are 1.5 to 2 times longer than their bodies.

6. The two eyeballs of a lizard are able to move in two different directions simultaneously.

7. When there is a shortage of water in their habitat, lizards save water in their body and excrete only salts.

8. Unlike what people think, chameleons change color in relation to their health, temperature, mood, communication, and light.

9. Most lizards don't have vocal cords, but Gecko Lizards are the only exception.

10. There are some species of lizards that squirt blood from their eyes when they face predators.

11. The largest lizard among all the species is the Komodo dragon.

Image of Komodo dragon

12. Lizards are found everywhere in the world except the continent of Antarctica.

13. There are many species of lizards and there are about 6263 species of lizards in this world.

14. Interestingly, among all the many species of lizards, only two of them are venomous.

15. The teeth of a lizard are replaced every time the earlier set of teeth fall off.

16. Lizards make use of their tongues to smell the air around them.

17. There are some species of lizards who look similar to snakes because they don't have legs or have small legs.

Image of Green And Brown Iguana

Rabbit Facts

1. Rabbits and guinea pigs don't always get along because their communication signals are misinterpreted.

2. Rabbits don't blink their eyes that much as they only blink 10 times an hour.

3. Rabbits chew anything that they can, so furniture and other things are kept away from them.

4. Rabbits are so fragile that they can be scared to death due to heart attacks.

5. Rabbits are able to sleep with their eyes open to look out for predators.

6. Rabbits usually run in a zigzag pattern to confuse predators and run away faster.

7. Rabbits in the wild don't live that much as they have a lifespan of around 2 years.

8. Rabbits have eyes on the sides of their head and this gives them almost a 360° view of their surroundings.

9. Rabbits are impressive jumpers as they can jump as high as 3 feet in the air and 10 feet forward.

10. Rabbits can rotate their ears 180 degrees to locate where a sound is coming from.

11. A baby rabbit shares the same name with a baby cat and is called a kitten or kitten.

12. Rabbits jump and sort of twist in the air whenever they are happy or excited.

13. Rabbit teeth never stop growing and they keep them down by using them on trees.

14. The only place rabbits are safest from predators is underground.

15. The ears of a rabbit help them to regulate their body temperatures.

Crocodile Facts

1. Crocodiles are pretty fast and their top speed is 22 miles per hour (35km/h).

2. There are not many species of crocodiles, as they are fourteen in number.

3. There are four species of crocodile that are endangered and they include Orinoco, Philippine, Cuban, and Siamese.

4. The lifespan of crocodiles varies depending on the species, and it ranges from 35 to 75 years.

5. The largest species of crocodiles is the saltwater crocodile which can grow up to 23 feet.

6. The smallest crocodile is a dwarf crocodile that only grows up to an average of 4.9 feet.

7. Crocodiles have the ability to hold their breath underwater for about an hour.

8. Crocodiles swallow small stones to help to enhance digestion.

9. Crocodiles cannot run much while they are on land reaching only 11 mph (17.7kph) for short distances.

10. Crocodiles don't have the ability to sweat.

11. Crocodiles keep themselves cool by opening their mouths once In a while.

12. The mouths of crocodiles are different from that of alligators because they are pointed and V-shaped.

13. The jaws of a crocodile are so powerful that they can exert 5,000 pounds of pressure per square inch.

14. Crocodiles grow a lot of teeth and can grow up to 4,000 teeth in their life.

15. A crocodile's bite is so strong that it is 10 times more powerful than that of a great white shark.

16. The longest crocodile that was captured alive measured 20.2 feet.

Giraffe Facts

1. Giraffes have a highly-specialized cardiovascular system (heart, veins, arteries, and capillaries) because of their unusual shape.

2. Giraffes get most of their water from their plant-based diet since they are easy prey when drinking from water sources.

3. The horns of a Giraffe are hair-covered and are called Ossicones.

4. Giraffes have jugular veins that contain a series of one-way valves that prevent excess blood from flowing to their brain.

5. The kick of a giraffe's long legs is able to inflict serious damage on a predator such as a lion or even kill them.

6. World giraffe day is celebrated on June 21st every year.

7. The heart of a giraffe is very large and it is two feet long and weighs up to 25 pounds (11.3kg).

8. Giraffes require over 75 pounds (34kg) of food a day and spend almost a greater part of the day eating.

9. Despite their characteristic long necks, giraffes only have seven vertebrae, the same as humans.

10. Giraffes usually stay upright while sleeping to prevent predators from catching up with them.

11. Giraffes' tongues are very long and can be up to 20 inches (0.51kg) long.

12. Giraffes are very fast and can run at speeds up to 35 mph (56.3kph) over short distances.

13. Giraffes only need to drink water once every couple of days since they depend on the leaves they eat to get water.

14. Female giraffes have the habit of returning to where they were born to give birth.

15. Giraffes have an unusual way of walking, by moving both legs on the same side of their body together.

Wolf Facts

1. Wolves are the largest member of the dog family and many of their species have gone extinct.

2. Wolves are social animals just like dogs and live in packs that can be up to 20.

3. Female wolves live in underground dens where they feed their newly born babies.

4. Howling is one of the major methods of communication for wolves.

5. Wolves have thick furs that help them to survive during the winter.

6. Wolves are fond of killing old, sick, or weak animals instead of killing agile and big ones.

7. Wolves can travel for long distances and can travel up to 124 miles (199.5km) in 24 hours.

8. Wolves eat a lot and can eat up to 9kg in a single sitting.

9. Wolves have long muzzles that end with a hyper-sensitive nose.

10. The hearing capacity of a wolf is twenty times better than human beings.

11. The howl of a single wolf is so loud that it can be heard up to ten kilometers.

12. A female wolf has a lot of pups and can have up to six pups in one breeding season.

13. The strongest male and female pairing lead the pack and are known as alphas.

14. A single wolf body measurement can be up to 5ft in length, standing at 3ft.

15. Wolves are estimated to live up to 13 years while they are not in the wild.

Butterfly Facts

1. The females of some butterfly species don't have wings, they move by crawling.

2. Butterflies make use of their feet to taste flowers and know where they can lay their eggs.

3. There are some species of butterflies that don't eat anything as adults and depend on what they ate as caterpillars to survive.

4. There are some species of butterflies that live up to some weeks or months while some last for a few hours.

5. The Monarch butterflies migrate from the Great Lakes to the Gulf of Mexico and return to the north again in the spring.

6. The Morgan's Sphinx Moth has a proboscis that is 12 (30.48cm) to 14 inches (35.56cm) long which they use to get the nectar.

7. There are numerous species of butterflies and there are up to 24,000 species.

8. Butterflies don't have the ability to fly if their body temperature is less than 86 degrees.

9. Butterflies have the ability to see colors such as red, green, and yellow.

10. Butterflies range in size depending on the species, from tiny 1/8 inch to a huge almost 12 inches (30.48cm).

11. There are some species of butterflies that can reach the speed of 15 miles per hour (24km/h).

12. The Brimstone butterfly is a species that has the longest lifetime of adult butterflies at 9-10 months.

13. The moths have numerous species at 140,000.

14. The red admiral butterfly communicates with each other through pheromones (pheromone is a chemical that an animal produces which changes the behavior of another animal of the same species).

15. There are some butterflies that have poisons due to the food they eat.

16. Butterflies can perceive colors outside of the human visual range, such as ultraviolet.

17. Monarch caterpillars are terrible pests and can devour a whole milkweed leaf within 6 minutes.

Pig Facts

1. A pig's sense of smell is around 2000 times better than human beings.

2. Pigs have a lot of population as there are around two billion pigs on earth.

3. If they are not living in the wild, pigs can live for up to 20 years.

4. Pigs like to build nests for any member of their family that is about to give birth.

5. Pigs are social animals and can form amazingly strong bonds with their family members.

6. Pigs use grunts and squeals to communicate and have over 20 vocalizations.

7. The baby pigs are born ready to run and walk, their eyes are open, unlike many animals.

8. The favorite way pigs like to sleep with their family members is nose to nose.

9. Pigs are very intelligent, more than dogs, and can remember things for years and years.

10. Pigs don't like loud noises around their environments such as yelling and dog barks.

11. Pigs are omnivore which means they can eat both plants and meat.

12. Piglets are super smart animals and can be trained to learn their names at just two weeks old.

13. Pigs like to roll in the mud because it helps to keep them cool.

14. Mother pigs have been known to do some kind of singing while they nurse their young.

15. Pigs are so brilliant that they designate a spot far away from their living and feeding areas as their toilet.

16. All pigs have the same ancestor, which is the Eurasian wild boar.

Dragon Facts

1. In China, there was a belief that emperors were descendants of dragons.

2. In Greek mythology, smaller dragons were often more fierce and deadly than large dragons.

3. In European folklore, the lance is the best weapon used for killing a dragon.

4. In Greek mythology, a female dragon is known as a drakaina.

5. In Greek mythology, the gods created dragons to watch treasures and wealth.

6. Dragons from Eastern cultures are more often depicted as kind, wise, and benevolent.

7. The home to the most places named after dragons in China.

8. It is said that the discoveries of dinosaur bones may have led people to believe in dragons.

9. Archaeologists have not found any proof that dragons ever existed.

10. Some scholars have traced the dragon myth to ancient Babylon, 4,000 years ago.

11. People who study dragons are known as dragonologist.

12. In China, dragons symbolize wealth, leadership, and authority.

13. Dragons from Western cultures typically are fire-breathing, evil, and symbolic of the battle between good and evil.

Dinosaur Facts

1. Scientists estimate that trillions of dinosaur eggs were laid during the Mesozoic period.

2. Tyrannosaurus rex ate so much meat that it was able to eat up to 22 tons of meat a year.

3. One of the fastest dinosaurs was Compsognathus and Ornithomimus.

4. Dinosaurs often swallowed large rocks which helped them to grind up food.

5. Liopleurodon was the biggest aquatic reptile and was half the size of a blue whale.

6. The smallest dinosaur skeleton ever found was that of Baby Mussaurus.

7. Tyrannosaurus rex had tiny front legs that were not much longer than human arms.

8. Small meat-eating dinosaurs may have been warm-blooded.

9. The Stegosaurus was the species that had the smallest brain for its body size of any recorded dinosaur.

10. Dinosaur eggs were so large that they were as large as basketballs.

11. The dinosaur that has the longest name is Micropachycephalosaurus.

12. Some of the skulls of a dinosaur were as long as a vehicle.

13. The bite of a T-rex was more than twice as powerful as that of a lion.

14. Dinosaurs lived on Earth for about 160 million years which is about 64 times the time humans have existed.

15. Triceratops is the species that had the biggest skull than any other dinosaur.

16. Dinosaurs lived in all parts of the world including Antarctica.

17. Brachiosaurus and Triceratops are dinosaurs that appeared during the Jurassic periods.

Chimpanzee Facts

A Chimpanzee

1. Groups of chimpanzees have been observed planning and executing raids on rival groups, similar to human warfare.

2. According to scientists, chimpanzees are human's closest relatives.

3. Although chimpanzees are omnivorous, only two percent of their diet consists of meat.

4. Chimpanzees can't swim although their homes are near water bodies.

5. Signs of Alzheimer's have been found in chimpanzees where their aged relatives tend to forget their families.

6. Chimps will warn each other if there is any sign of danger.

7. Just like human beings, chimpanzees sleep for 8-9 hours a night.

8. Chimps can be infected with the same illnesses as humans such as Ebola, dementia, etc.

9. Female chimpanzees don't give birth that much as they will have an average of 3 infants in their lifetime.

10. Chimps have been observed to have empathy for other species of animals just like humans.

11. Chimpanzees are social animals and their communities may consist of over 100 chimpanzees with a hierarchy.

12. Chimps are one of the few animals that can use tools such as stones and sticks.

13. Chimpanzees can make over 30 different noises to communicate with each other.

14. Chimpanzees can also run very fast and can move up to speeds of 25mph (40.2kph).

15. Just like humans, chimpanzees have senses similar to the five senses humans have.

16. Africa is the only place in the world where wild chimpanzees are found.

17. Chimpanzees share about 98.7% of their DNA with humans.

Monkey Facts

A Monkey

1. Mandrill monkeys are known to have fangs (long, pointed teeth) that are longer than that of a lion.

2. The tip of a monkey's tail is a patch of bare skin that is very unique just like human fingerprints.

3. The capuchin monkey is the most intelligent of the New World monkeys.

4. The most acrobatic of the New World monkeys are the spider monkey.

5. Old World Monkeys are Monkeys that live in Africa and Asia continents.

6. New World Monkeys are monkeys that live in Central and South America.

7. Among all the New World Monkeys, uakari is one of the most unusual-looking.

8. The fastest monkey on Earth is the Patas monkey which can reach up to 34 miles (54.7km) per hour.

9. The monkey with the longest tail is the female spider monkey.

10. Diseases that can spread from monkeys to humans such as yellow fever, Ebola, etc.

11. With a 5 inches (12.7cm) body, the smallest monkey in the world is the pygmy marmoset.

12. According to scientists, female monkeys can teach their young how to floss their teeth.

13. Monkeys are so intelligent that they can understand written numbers.

14. Male monkeys urinate in their hands and then rub it thoroughly into their fur to attract females.

15. The owl monkey is the only nocturnal New World monkey.

Gorilla Facts

A Gorilla

1. Gorillas have the ability to depend on the leaves they eat as their source of water.

2. An adult male gorilla eats a lot and can eat up to 40 pounds (18.1kg) of veggies each day.

3. The pregnancy period of female gorillas is almost the same as humans at 8.5 months.

4. Gorillas are not a good match for humans as they are roughly six times stronger than the average human.

5. The arms of gorillas are longer than their legs which makes them walk on all four most of the time.

6. Gorillas are pretty tall and are between four and six feet tall when standing.

7. Cross River Gorillas are one of the world's most critically endangered primates.

8. There are two species of gorillas, the Eastern and Western species.

9. Although they walk on all fours most of the time, gorillas can walk upright on two legs.

10. Gorilla's hands have opposable thumbs, just like human beings.

11. Gorillas can learn sign language and make use of rudimentary tools.

12. Gorilla's life span can be up to 50 to 60 years in captivity and 35 years in the wild.

13. Gorillas are the closest primate to humans after chimpanzees and bamboos.

14. Gorillas have impressive language skills and can communicate with each other using them.

15. Gorillas rank amongst the most recognized primates in the world.

Physical and Behavioral Differences Apes

In this chapter, we will highlight the physical and behavioral differences baboon, monkey, orangutan, gorilla, and chimpanzee.

Facial Features of Apes:

Baboons

Baboons have long, dog-like snouts with prominent canines and bony brow ridges that give them a fierce appearance.

Monkeys

Monkeys display a wide variety of facial features, with some having flat faces and others elongated muzzles, depending on the species.

Orangutans

Male orangutans develop large cheek pads with wide, flat faces and small noses, which signify dominance.

Gorillas

Gorillas have flat, wide faces with large nostrils and prominent brow ridges, giving them a powerful yet gentle expression.

Chimpanzees

Chimpanzees have flatter faces with pronounced brow ridges and expressive eyes that reflect their highly social nature.

Tail:

Most monkeys have tails, which are often prehensile (can grasp) in species like the spider monkey.

Baboons, Orangutans, Gorillas, and Chimpanzees do not have tails. This is a key distinction between monkeys and apes.

Locomotion:

Monkeys are primarily quadrupedal, using all four limbs to move across branches or the ground.

Baboons walk on all fours (quadrupedal), but more often on the ground than in trees.

Orangutans are arboreal apes (tree-dwelling) and move by brachiation (swinging from branch to branch) and climbing.

Gorillas and Chimpanzees are walk quadrupedally ape but use knuckle-walking (walking on the knuckles of their forelimbs).

Body Size:

Baboons and Monkeys are generally smaller compared to the great apes, though baboons are larger than most monkeys.

Orangutans are large, with males reaching up to 200 pounds (90 kg).

Gorillas are the largest primates, with males weighing up to 500 pounds (230 kg).

Chimpanzees are smaller than gorillas and orangutans, males weighing around 130 pounds (60 kg).

Habitat:

Monkeys and Baboons are mostly found in various regions across Africa, Asia, and South America. Baboons prefer savannas and open grasslands, while monkeys can be arboreal.

Orangutans are native to the rainforests of Borneo and Sumatra in Southeast Asia.

Gorillas and Chimpanzees are native to the forests and mountains of Central Africa.

Diet:

Monkeys eat fruits, leaves, insects, and small animals, with variation depending on the species.

Baboons are Omnivores, known to eat a wide variety of foods, including grass, fruits, seeds, and even small mammals.

Orangutans are primarily frugivores (fruit-eaters), but they also eat leaves and bark.

Gorillas are herbivorous, eating leaves, stems, bamboo, and fruit.

Chimpanzees are omnivores, with a diet of fruits, leaves, and sometimes hunting small animals or other primates.

Social Structure:

Monkeys and Baboons live in large, complex social groups with hierarchies, especially baboons, who have strict dominance rankings.

Orangutans are Solitary animals, with males and females mostly living apart except during mating periods.

Gorillas live in troops led by a dominant silverback male, usually consisting of several females and their offspring.

Chimpanzees live in large, social groups with intricate relationships, often dominated by alpha males.

Tool Use:

Some Monkeys species, like capuchin monkeys, use tools (e.g., rocks to crack nuts).

Baboons are rarely use tools.

Orangutans, Gorillas, and Chimpanzees are known for advanced tool use, with chimpanzees being especially proficient (e.g., using sticks to fish for termites).

Facial Expressions:

Monkeys and Baboons have a range of facial expressions, though not as complex as those of great apes.

Orangutans, Gorillas, and Chimpanzees display a wide variety of facial expressions similar to humans, indicating emotions like joy, fear, and anger.

Communication:

Monkeys rely heavily on vocalizations and gestures to communicate within their groups.

Baboons use vocal calls, facial expressions, and body language to maintain social order.

Orangutans use long calls to communicate across distances, especially by males.

Gorillas use grunts, chest-beating, and body postures to communicate.

Chimpanzees are Very vocal, using screams, hoots, and gestures to communicate complex ideas.

Parental Care:

Monkeys and Baboons mothers primarily take care of the young, but baboons live in multi-male, multi-female troops where infants are often groomed by others.

Orangutans have the longest dependence period among apes, with young staying with their mothers for up to 8 years.

Gorilla females care for the young, but the dominant male silverback also plays a protective role.

Chimpanzee mothers provide long-term care, with young chimpanzees staying with them for several years.

Intelligence:

Monkeys and Baboons are Intelligent, with some species showing problem-solving skills, though not as advanced as great apes.

Orangutans, Gorillas, and Chimpanzees are highly intelligent, especially chimpanzees and orangutans, known for complex tool use, communication, and social learning.

Physical Strength:

Baboons are quite stronger than monkeys but both are weaker compared to apes.

Orangutans, Gorillas, and Chimpanzees very strong, with orangutans and gorillas being especially powerful. A chimpanzee's strength is also notable, being much stronger than humans of the same weight.

Lifespan:

Monkeys and Baboons live up to 20-30 years.

Orangutans, Gorillas, and Chimpanzees can live up to 40-50 years in the wild and longer in captivity.

Aggression:

Baboons can be very aggressive, especially males fighting for dominance.

Orangutans are generally solitary and non-aggressive, except during mating disputes.

Gorillas are peaceful, but the silverback will show aggression to protect the troop.

Chimpanzees are known for violent behavior, including group warfare and hunting.

Arms and Legs:

Monkeys and Baboons have arms and legs of similar length, adapted for quadrupedal movement.

Orangutans, Gorillas, and Chimpanzees have longer arms compared to legs, aiding in climbing and brachiation.

Orangutan Facts

1. Orangutans are known to share 28 distinct physical characteristics with humans.

2. There are two species of orangutans and they include the Sumatran Orangutan and the Borneo Orangutan.

3. Sumatran Orangutans are thinner than Borneo Orangutans.

4. Female orangutans have their first infant between 12 and 15 years of age.

5. Orangutans are also very good observers of human behavior and are known to imitate washing of clothes, making use of nails, etc.

6. Orangutan howls are so loud that it can reach over 1km through the forest canopy.

7. Orangutans are so brilliant that they have been taught American Sign Language.

8. Orangutans are currently considered highly endangered because of the loss of habitat and poaching.

9. Orangutans have an enormous arm span that can reach up to 8 feet.

10. Orangutans give birth every 7-8 years after their first child.

11. Orangutans are renowned for their high intelligence and are known to make use of tools that are more complex.

12. Orangutans have been shown to display individual personalities in a group of orangutans.

13. Orangutans are more solitary than other great ape species.

14. According to scientists, orangutans diverged from the other apes over 10-16 million years ago.

15. Orangutans have one of the most prolonged developments of any mammal as they depend on their mother most of the time.

16. Orangutans have been known to show signs of empathy for other species of animals.

Baboon Facts

1. Baboons are not able to make use of tools like other primates like monkeys.

2. Baboons threaten each other with yawns that display their canine teeth.

3. Baboons don't spend most of their time on trees, but on the ground.

4. Baboons prefer to sleep in an upright seated position on a tree branch.

5. Baboons have cheek pouches where they smuggle some foods they don't want to eat right away.

6. Baboons can also give little lessons to groups of youngsters in their troops.

7. Female baboons are pregnant for 6 months and give birth to mostly one offspring.

8. Baboons are promiscuous and males and females can have different partners.

9. Adult male baboons are usually twice as large as adult female baboons.

10. Baboons stare into each other's eyes and are one of the few animals to do so.

11. The tails of a baboon cannot assist them in climbing trees.

12. Baboons are very vocal and have about 40 different distinct vocalizations.

13. Baboons have long dog-like snouts and they walk like dogs too.

14. Baboons are native to Africa and some areas of the Asia continent.

15. Baboons are very social animals and they live in large groups, up to 100 baboons.

16. Baboons are one of the largest monkey species and have just a stump of a tail.

100 General Snake Facts

1. There are many species of snakes, about three thousand six hundred species.

2. There are only six countries in the world that don't have snakes and they include New Zealand, Iceland, Greenland, Cape Verde, Ireland, and Antarctica.

3. You can know if a snake is a venomous snake or not by looking at its eyes.

4. Interestingly, snakes with slitted or elliptical pupils are venomous while those with round eyelids are not.

5. Snakes that live in the wild can reach an average age of 100 while those in captivity are able to live up to 170 years.

6. The existence of snakes can be dated back to ninety-eight million years ago.

7. Snake scales help them to breathe while they are in the water.

8. The scales of a snake also help them to retain moisture in their body.

9. Mongoose has developed immunity that helps them to withstand the venom of a snake.

10. The bones that make up the snake skeleton are between the ranges of 600 to 1800 bones depending on the snake.

11. Interestingly, snakes have about ten bones from their skill to their jaw.

12. Not every snake lays eggs, about 70 percent lay eggs while 30 percent give birth to their young lives.

13. The venom that comes from the Pico jackfruit snake is capable of curing cancer.

14. Albino snakes are more vulnerable to the sun's light since they are sensitive to UV rays.

15. Denim is capable of stopping about 60 to 66 percent of a snake's venom if you are bitten while wearing them.

16. Snakes don't use their teeth to chew, rather they use them to hold their prey.

17. Unlike most animals' teeth, the teeth of a snake are curved backward.

18. Snakes make use of their venom to immobilize prey and also to digest them after swallowing.

19. There are about 20 different compounds of proteins and polypeptides that make up the snake venom.

20. Snakes and birds have one thing in common and it is that their poop looks almost the same.

21. Unlike human beings and some other animals, the skin of a snake is not flexible.

22. Interestingly, snakes shed and molt their skin about three to six times in a year.

23. Snakes make use of rough objects around them to trigger the shedding process of their skin.

24. The Ilha da Queimada Grande is an island in Brazil that is just filled with snakes.

25. The hedgehog has developed immunity against the venom of snakes.

26. Snakes are known as opportunists while hunting and they eat about six to thirty times a year.

27. Interestingly, snakes are able to slow their metabolism to about 70 percent.

28. Scale less snakes are more favorites to be pets than snakes with scales.

29. The flying snakes don't fly unlike what people think, rather they glide through trees.

Image of flying snake

30. The Arafura file snake lays only one egg only once every decade.

31. A lot of people have fear of snakes and about one in every three adults is afraid of snakes.

32. The largest fossil of a snake that has been found is that of the Titanoboa, which is about 50ft. long.

33. The most venomous snake in the world is the Inland taipan whose venom is capable of killing 100 men and 2500 mice.

Image of Inland taipan

34. The fastest snake in the world moves about 4.32 to 5.4 meters per second, and it is the black mamba.

35. The Black mamba is one of the most venomous snakes and kills about 20,000 people a year in Africa.

36. With 21 species out of the 23 known species of deadly snakes, Australia has the most dangerous species of snakes.

37. The snake that strikes the fastest is not the black mamba, rather it is the death adder.

Image of black mamba

38. When a snake wants to eat its body size can stretch multiple times to accommodate the food.

39. Interestingly, snakes are Able to eat prey that is 75 to 100 percent bigger than them.

40. Snakes make use of their throat to pump water into their stomach.

41. Because of their poor eyesight, most snakes make use of their tongue to navigate.

42. The fangs of a snake last for about six to ten weeks before it falls off.

43. The jaws of a snake is not fixed to their jaws, rather it is ligaments that connect them to their skull.

44. The Mozambique spitting cobra has permanent blinding venom and can spit from any angle.

45. Interestingly, snakes are able to open their mouths 150 degrees to swallow their prey.

46. The amount of offspring that a snake has depends on the amount of food that they eat, the more a snake eats the more it has offspring.

47. Snakes are not able to generate their own body heat since they are cold-blooded.

48. Interestingly, the body system of a snake will fail whenever the temperature is below 10 degrees Celsius.

49. Some snakes such as the non-venomous are able to fold back their fangs to the roof of their mouth.

50. Heat is one of the things that trigger the hunger instincts of a snake.

51. When a snake is not able to eat or find prey, it starts to eat itself and will eventually die.

52. The growth rate of a snake decreases as it starts to age, but a snake does not stop growing.

53. The snake that is the most endangered on earth is the St Lucia racer.

54. The recorded cases of snake casualties are about forty thousand people.

55. Half of the snake casualties that are recorded in the world are in India.

56. The venom of a species of snake does not affect it since they commonly bite each other during mating.

57. The secretary bird is one of the few animals that have an immune system that can withstand snake venom.

58. When a snake bites another one of another species, it can result in the death of the snake if the other one is venomous.

59. One of the most intelligent snakes in the world is the king cobra since it has a strong familial sense.

60. Some snakes that live in the sea are able to dive about 300 feet into the sea.

61. Sea snakes, unlike what people think, do not have gills and need to surface from time to time to take a breath.

62. Unlike most animals, snakes don't have external ears, rather they have inner ears.

63. The most common snake in the world is the garter snake which is often bought as a pet.

64. Lemongrass and mothballs act as snake repellent and can keep snakes away from your surroundings.

65. Because of their low metabolism rate, the organs of a snake have the ability to live longer.

66. Interestingly, the head of a snake can still bite after being cut off and it is even more fatal.

67. In North America, the only water venomous snake is the cottonmouth snake.

68. The Mozambique spitting cobra is known to have a 100 percent spitting accuracy and spot from eight feet away.

Image of spitting cobra

69. One of the weirdest snake facts is that the Sonoran Coral snake releases a fart whenever it is scared.

70. Snakes don't have eyelids, so they are not able to blink like some other animals.

71. The pine snake spends the winters, hot summers, and most of its time underground.

72. Unlike the eggs of a bird, the eggs of a snake are leathery and are able to expand to accommodate its young.

73. Although they are classified as constrictors, the black racer snake does not constrict.

74. Some snakes such as the python and the boa do not hibernate like other snakes.

75. Reaching up to 16 to 23 feet long, pythons are not venomous, rather they kill their prey by suffocating them.

76. There is no snake that is an herbivore, all of them are carnivores.

77. There is a wine in Vietnam that is made of the blood of a cobra snake.

78. When a snake feels threatened after a meal, it can throw up the food to enable it to fight.

79. In the past, the black mamba used to have a hundred percent fatality rate before anti-venom was made.

80. The tail muscles of rattlesnakes are one of the fastest muscles of animals in the world.

81. The venom of newborn snakes is just as deadly as that of adult snakes.

82. By digesting its organs one after the other, a snake is able to live for two years without food.

83. Elephant trunk snakes are almost completely aquatic snake species.

84. A snake's digestive system can dissolve everything except the hair, feathers, and claws of its prey.

85. The Gabon viper has the longest fangs of any snake, reaching about 2 inches (5.08cm).

86. Larger snakes, such as boas, have heat-sensing organs called labial pits in front of their mouth.

87. Snakes do not lap up water as mammals do.

88. A snake's fangs usually last about 6–10 weeks before it is replaced with another one.

89. The snake forked tongue tips taste different amounts of chemicals.

90. Scales cover every inch of a snake's body, even its eyes.

91. The most common snake in North America is the garter snake.

92. Rattlesnake rattles are made of rings of keratin, and this is the same material that makes up human hair and fingernails.

Image of a Rattlesnake

93. Although they are venomous snakes, the inland taipan is actually quite shy and placid.

94. To avoid predators, some snakes can poop whenever they want to be smelly.

95. The warmer a snake's body, the more quickly it can digest its prey.

96. The fear of snakes is one of the most common phobias worldwide.

97. The Brahminy Blind Snake is the only species of snake that is solely female.

98. Some species of snakes have over two hundred teeth.

99. Some snakes, such as pythons and boas, still have traces of back legs in their body.

100. Snakes evolved from a four-legged reptilian ancestor according to scientists.

Thank you so much for purchasing this book and making it this far in the book!

I greatly appreciate the time your kid is taking to read the facts in this book.

As a small publisher, knowing that this book is both fun and educational to your kid, means a lot to me.

If you have 60 seconds, hearing your honest feedback on Amazon about what your kid thinks of this book, would mean the world to me.

It does wonders for the book, I love hearing about your kid's experience with the book.

How to leave a feedback:

- Open your camera app or QR code Scanner.

- Point your mobile device at the QR code below

- The review page will appear in your web browser.

OR Visit: funsided.com/FAK

Python Facts

1. Unlike what people think, pythons are non-venomous snakes.

2. Because they are not native to South or North America, they are classified as old-world snakes.

3. According to the Reptile Database, there are about 41 species of pythons.

4. Some of the world's largest snakes are python species as they can grow up to 30 feet.

5. The smallest species of pythons are the anthill pythons which only grow about 2 feet.

6. The major constituents of python food include Rodents, birds, and monkeys.

7. The average litter size of a python is thirty-five eggs.

8. The average length of python species is between two to thirty feet.

9. The habitat of pythons includes grasslands, woodlands, swamps, rocky outcrops, dunes, and shrubs.

10. The population of pythons is estimated to be between 30,000 and 300,000

11. Pythons are solitary animals and prefer to live on their own and usually come together to mate.

12. Pythons are oviparous, which means they are among the snake species that lay eggs.

13. Pythons are known to live more than two decades while in captivity.

14. The longest living species of pythons is the ball python which can live up to 40 years.

15. Female pythons do not eat when they are incubating their eggs.

16. Pythons make use of chemicals from their body to communicate their gender, age, and condition of reproduction with other snakes that are present in their surroundings.

King Cobra Facts

1. The largest venomous snake in the whole world is the King cobra.

2. The venom of a king cobra is strong enough to kill twenty humans and 1 elephant.

3. King cobras never stop growing and can grow up to 10 to 13 feet in length.

4. Because of how long it is, king cobras need to shed their skin five times a year.

5. The reason why King cobras shed their skin 5 times a year is to accommodate the prey they swallow.

6. King cobras can climb trees better than humans and can climb up a 65 feet tree.

7. To swim, king cobras need to flatten their bodies and they can swim faster than humans.

8. King cobras are known to eat their fellow snakes such as rat snakes as their food.

9. King cobras eat the head of their prey first before swallowing the body.

10. King cobras are the sole member of their genus and they are no other subspecies.

11. King cobras are the only species of cobras that don't spit venom, rather they inject them when they bite.

12. King cobras are equipped with an exceptional nervous system that helps them to hunt prey.

13. King cobras are recognized as the most brilliant snake species in the world.

14. King cobra snakes and other cobras can't hear the music of a snake charmer's flute.

15. Baby cobras are able to produce venom immediately after they are born.

Viper Facts

1. Viper species are found all over the world except for Antarctica.

2. Vipers engage in a hunting activity called prey relocation where they bite their prey and allow them to die before tracing them down to eat.

3. The diet of vipers includes small mammals, birds, lizards, and eggs.

4. Africa's puff adders are very fast and can strike at a speed of a quarter of a second.

5. Vipers can extend their fangs and bite without injecting venom.

6. Vipers are known to detect the location of their prey chemically.

7. Vipers prefer to depend on their camouflage for protection rather than their ability to move fast.

8. The habitat of vipers ranges from living in mountains, rainforests, fields, and deserts.

9. The mouth of vipers can open nearly 180 degrees.

10. Vipers can rotate their fangs together or independently.

11. Most vipers have keeled scales, coloring, and patterns that serve as camouflage.

12. The longest venomous snake in the Americas is the South American Bushmaster.

13. Almost all vipers are known to have a distinctive triangular head.

14. The smallest viper in the world is the Mao-Lan pit viper.

15. Vipers found in colder, northern climates have more moderate venom.

Anaconda Facts

1. The four species of anaconda in the world are green anaconda, the yellow or Paraguayan anaconda, the dark-spotted anaconda and the Beni or Bolivian anaconda.

2. Anacondas are not found everywhere in the world as they are known to be dominant in South America in the wild.

3. Anacondas are very large animals and can reach up to 40 feet in length.

4. Anacondas are semi-aquatic which means they can live on water and land.

5. Anacondas are not related to pythons as people think, but they are both constrictors.

6. The heaviest snake in the world is the green anaconda.

7. Their eyes that are fixed on top of the anaconda's head allow them to see above the water while remaining mostly submerged.

8. Anacondas are thick and muscular snakes that are thicker than bats.

9. Although anacondas are not poisonous, their bite may be quite painful.

10. The scales of an anaconda are built to allow for the absorption of water.

11. Female anacondas are larger and longer than males.

12. The coloring and size of anacondas depend on their species.

13. The average size of female anacondas is around 15 feet while the males are 9 feet.

14. The estimated weight of anacondas is around 25p kilograms.

15. Anacondas can swim very well and can swim very much faster than human beings.

16. Anacondas just like other snakes are solitary and prefer to be on their own.

17. Anacondas don't lay eggs and give birth to their offspring alive.

100 General Fish Facts

1. The Largest fish in the world is nearly 16 meters long, and this is the whale Shark.

2. Not every animal that is called a fish such as a jellyfish, starfish, is really fish

Picture of a starfish

3. Inside the water, fish do not breathe, they filter the dissolved oxygen that is in the water.

4. There are fishes that have some warm-blooded characteristics, such as whale fish and tuna.

5. Unlike what many people believe, there are some species of fishes that lay their eggs on land instead of the water, such as the mudskipper.

6. There are two main water environments that fishes live in, and there are saltwater and freshwater.

7. Scientists have some theories on how the first species of fishes evolved from sea squirts.

8. Interestingly, the earliest species of fishes did not have jaws, and there are still some fishes such as the lampreys or long, eel-like fishes.

9. The only species of fishes in the world that are lobe-finned are coelacanth and lungfishes.

10. The lungfish doesn't function like most fishes; it has to come to the surface to take some air before diving in again.

11. Interestingly, lungfishes are able to slow their metabolism rate to 1/80 of the normal metabolism.

12. Eels and mudskippers are able to breathe air into their body by making use of their skin.

Image of a Mudskippers fish

13. The brain of an average fish when compared to a bird's brain is like 1/15; there are exceptions to this.

14. There are some daytime fishes that see better than human beings with good vision.

15. Interestingly, the nocturnal fishes have a below-average daytime vision but see well in the dark than humans.

16. The major organs that most fishes make use of are; the heart, their skeleton, and their ear.

17. Instead of laying eggs, there are some sharks that carry and give birth to their young ones.

18. Fishes are able to produce sounds on their own by rubbing their bones together.

19. Interestingly there are a few others that make use of their swim bladder to send communication signals.

20. The slime or mucus that is found in the body of fish is used by them to prevent diseases by trapping microorganisms.

21. If fish stay out at the surface of the water for too long in the very hot sun, they may get sunburns.

22. Fishes make use of counter shading to shift colors all over their body, from dark colors at the head to lighter ones at the tail side.

23. How the immune system of fishes functions is similar to that of human beings.

24. Fishes such as the Bluestreak cleaner wrasse are known as cleaner fishes for their ability to eat parasites out of other fish bodies.

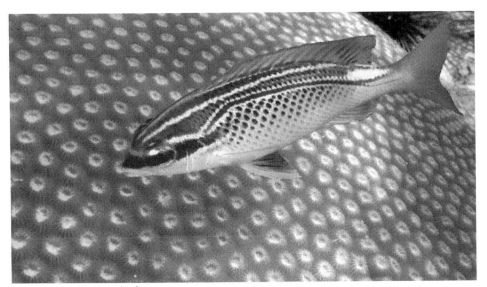

Image of a Bluestreak cleaner

25. The only fish in the animal kingdom that has eyelids are the sharks.

26. Fishes make use of their swim bladders to provide balance inside the water.

27. Interestingly, fish species such as sharks and rays do not have swim bladders and that is why they swim even while sleeping.

28. Electric eels exude a lot of power and can release up to a full ampere of electricity.

29. The fish with the most deadly poison in the world is the stonefish.

30. Since the poison of stonefish is heat-sensitive, it is possible to eat stonefish.

31. Interestingly, unlike the stonefish, the putter fish is still deadly to eat even after heating.

Image of a stonefish

32. Male Emperor Angelfish have about 4 to 6 female fishes of the same species in their harem.

33. The female Emperor angelfish is able to change its gender from the female gender to the male gender when the leader of the harem dies.

34. Unlike what people think, flying fish don't actually fly, they only glide in the air.

35. Flying fishes are also able to reach an impressive height of 6 meters.

36. Piranha has very sharp teeth that are able to tear away flesh, although there are no records of eating people.

37. The seahorses are the only species of fish that are able to swim in an upright position, which makes them slow.

38. Salmons are very impressive swimmers, they are able to swim about 3,200 km in just 60 days.

39. The male seahorses are the ones that carry the eggs instead of the females in their pouch.

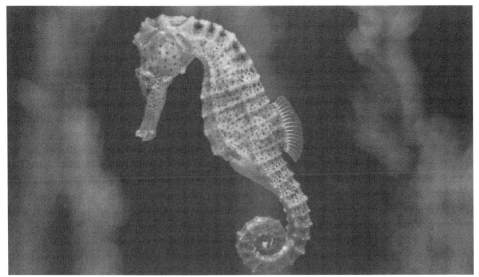

Image of a Seahorses

40. Clownfish make use of their colors to protect themselves from predators.

41. When a fish is sleeping, their brain activity is different from that of humans.

42. The Antarctic fish is capable of living below freezing temperature because they have antifreeze in their blood.

43. One can determine if a fish can move very fast or slow by looking at its fins and tail.

44. In a school of fishes, there is one leader and the leader stays in the center of the school.

45. The majority of fishes are only able to swim forward and not backward except species like eels.

46. Tetra pods, which include vertebrates, evolved from fishes according to scientists.

47. The smell of fish that our nose picks up doesn't come from the fish, but as a result of staying outside the water.

48. About 154 million tons is the average tons of fish that are caught every year in the fishing industry.

49. Fishes that are released back into the water after they have been caught, don't live long.

50. Only about 1% of the whole fishing ecosystem has been studied by scientists.

51. Most fish can see in color and use colors to camouflage themselves.

52. A fish does not add new scales as it grows, but the size of its scales increases as they grow.

53. An inflated porcupine fish can reach a diameter of up to 35 inches (88.9cm).

Image of porcupine fish

54. Fangtooth teeth are so big that they can't close their mouths completely.

55. The fish in the middle of a school is the one that controls the school.

56. The fastest fish is the sailfish and it can swim as fast as a car on a highway.

57. The slowest fish is a seahorse and it is so slow that you can barely see it moving.

58. A Fish will suffocate if it tries to chew since it would interfere with water passing over its gills.

59. The strongest female fish swims in the middle of the school.

60. The mudskipper fish spends most of its time out of the water and can "walk" on its fins.

61. The batfish plays dead when danger or a predator is near.

Image of a batfish

62. Hammerhead sharks can live in schools of more than five hundred sharks.

63. Anableps is a four-eyed fish that can see above and below the water simultaneously.

64. The light of a female angler is always on.

65. The entire body of a catfish is covered with taste buds.

66. An Atlantic hagfish can make enough slime in one minute to fill a bucket.

67. A seahorse has the ability to move each of its eyes separately.

68. An Australian lungfish in an aquarium in Chicago managed to live for 84 years.

Image of a lungfish

69. Salmon can adapt to live in rivers, lakes, estuaries, coral reefs, and the open sea.

70. Female seahorses lay their eggs inside a pouch on the male seahorse's belly.

71. Lampreys fish are classified as pests in North America.

72. The ocean sunfish does not have a tail like other fishes.

73. Some fishes have warm-blooded traits such as sharks.

74. Fish immune systems work like human beings.

75. Male anglerfish are much smaller than the female in body structure.

Image of an anglerfish

76. Seahorses can also change their color to match their surroundings.

77. The number of people who fish for sport in the United States is about 40 million.

78. Pufferfish chefs have a license of their own because of how lethal their poisons can be.

79. Overfishing also causes clashes between various groups.

80. Mudskippers fish have the ability to jump 2 feet in the air.

81. Hagfish are some of the slimiest animals in the world.

82. Lampreys are jawless and have a round sucker-like mouth.

83. According to scientists, the first jawed fishes didn't have teeth.

84. Lampreys and hagfish are the most primitive form of fish still in existence.

Image of Lampreys

85. A female sunfish can lay 300 million eggs each year.

86. Lungfishes can live for a very long time.

87. Rice fish from Thailand all reach a maximum length of 0.5 inches (1.27cm) which is roughly the size of a grain of rice.

88. The oils and alcohols in the coelacanth flesh make their flavor unpleasant.

89. Swimmers don't notice the stonefish until its spines sting them.

90. Seahorses swim upright and they are the only fish that do so.

91. It's impossible to completely remove the poison from a puffer fish's flesh.

92. Fish tornadoes are a rare natural phenomenon that takes fish into the air and brings them down when the tornado stops.

93. Sea anemones deliver painful stings that can be fatal to fish.

94. Fishes that have thin fins and a split tail move fast and can swim long distances.

95. Electric eels have the ability to swim backward.

96. Spending too much time out of the water before returning to it can cause stress to fish.

97. Some forms of fishing can harm the environment such as the use of chemicals.

98. Hagfish have the ability to absorb organic compounds through their skin.

99. Empty dogfish egg cases sometimes wash up on the beach.

100. While sleeping, the brain activity of a fish doesn't shift the way humans do.

Shark Facts

Image of Great White Shark

1. The embryos of a shark are known to attack each other.

2. Female sharks can reproduce without mating with male sharks.

3. Bull shark jaws work the same way that a vice operates.

4. Hippopotamus, deer, and cows are more deadly than sharks in terms of deaths.

5. Great whites do specialize in sneak attacks and allow their prey to bleed to death before eating them.

6. The bull shark has the strongest bite of a shark, with a force of 478 pounds (216.8kg).

Image of a Bull shark

7. Hammerheads are known to have a 360-degree vision because of the shape of their head.

8. Great whites have a more powerful bite than that of a wild cat.

9. Some shark species are pregnant for a long time, up to two years.

10. There are many types of sharks, up to five hundred species of them.

11. Female sharks are considerably larger in size than male sharks.

12. There are few species of shark that are known to inhabit freshwater lakes and rivers like the bull shark.

13. Whale sharks have been known to give a ride to a swimmer.

14. The longest fish in the world is a species of shark.

15. Hammerhead sharks have a whopping 3,000 ampullary pores for picking up electrical fields in the water.

Dolphin Facts

Image of a Dolphin

1. The lifespan of a dolphin is solely dependent on the species.

2. Unlike sharks, dolphins are known to have a very poor sense of smell.

3. There are about five species of dolphins that live in freshwater.

4. Dolphins make use of echolocation to find the location of their prey.

5. Dolphins are mammals like humans and give birth to their young ones alive.

6. Bottlenose dolphins are known to live in tropical and temperate waters.

7. Dolphins make use of specific individual whistles in order to identify each other.

8. Dolphins have two stomachs, one is used for storage, and the other one for digestion.

9. When dolphins are sleeping, half of their brain is not sleeping so that they can continue to breathe.

10. Dolphins are known to take care of their family members in case they are sick or about to die.

11. Dolphins are very intelligent and can be trained to perform different athletic skills.

12. Dolphins are carnivorous animals and they don't chew their food.

13. Dolphins are not solitary animals and they live in a group of 2 to 40 members known as pods.

14. The sense of hearing of dolphins is about ten times better than human beings.

15. When making use of echolocation, it is the teeth of dolphins that pick up the echoes.

16. The dorsal fins of dolphins are unique, just like human fingerprints.

17. Dolphins hold their breath for long periods of time up to 30 minutes.

18. Dolphin eyes can move separately from one other.

19. Dolphins are the only mammals that give birth to their young ones' tails first.

105 General Bird Facts

1. Tropical rainforests are home to most species of birds, 2 out of 3 species of birds live in the tropical rainforest.

2. The only bird whose beak is bigger than the body is the Sword-billed Hummingbird.

Image of Hummingbird

3. Soft fringes on owl's wings make their flight not as noisy as other birds.

4. There are 30 categories of birds and about nine thousand five hundred species of them.

5. The beak of a pelican is able to reach about two feet, making it the longest in the world.

6. Hummingbirds are the only birds that can fly backwards in the world.

7. Unlike some animals, birds do not have bladders to store their urine.

8. Interestingly, the ostrich has a separation of urine and feces, unlike some other birds.

9. Coal Miners in the past often used a bird called canary to detect poisonous levels of carbon monoxide gas.

An image of a canary bird

10. The hoatzin chicks have two claws on their wings which they use to climb in mangrove trees.

11. Measuring 34.7 feet, the longest feathers of a bird was that of a chicken in Japan.

12. The lungs of a bird are more efficient and take up more space than that of a mammal.

13. Owls cannot swivel their eyes, they move their heads completely around to see what's behind them.

14. Unlike what people think, Ostriches do not bury their heads in the sand when danger is near.

15. The only bird with its nostrils at the end of its beak is the kiwi and it helps them to sniff food.

16. The bird that lays the smallest egg in the world is the bee hummingbird.

17. The most talkative bird in the world is the African gray parrot which can say over 800 words.

18. The pink colors that flamingos have are from the beta-carotene in their crustacean and plankton diet.

An Image of flamingos

19. With echolocation, bats are able to fly through a moving fan.

20. The most common wild bird is the red-billed Quelea, with a breeding population of 1.4 billion pairs.

21. There are some birds that sing notes too high for humans to hear such as starlings.

22. There are some bird nests that have been in existence for over a hundred years.

23. The ostrich lays the biggest egg in the world and its eggs can weigh up to 3 pounds (1.4kg).

24. Unlike some other birds with many feathers, hummingbirds have as many as just 1000 feathers.

25. A woodpecker will drum its beak against a tree instead of singing like other birds.

Image of a woodpecker

26. The Gentoo Penguins are the fastest birds that swim and can reach speeds of 22 mph (35.4kph).

27. Oil birds are the only bird species that use echolocation the way that bats do.

28. A green woodpecker eats many ants per day and can eat as many as 2,000 ants per day.

29. The song of a European wren can be heard 1,650 feet away.

30. The feathers of a bird weigh more than its skeleton.

31. The chicks of large bird species often take the longest to hatch while the smallest take the shortest time.

32. One of the rarest birds in the world is the Japanese crested ibis.

Image of Japanese crested ibis

33. The bird with the most feathers in the world is the whistling swan, with up to 25,000 feathers.

34. The marsh warbler is a mimic bird that can mimic more than 80 different birds.

35. Approximately 75% of birds that live in the wild live for less than a year.

36. A pelican's pouch-like beak can hold up to 2.5 liters of water at a time.

37. Some bird nests can weigh a few tons and have over 300 birds living in them.

38. The heaviest bird of prey is the Andean condor and it can weigh up to 12 kg.

Image of Andean condor

39. Oil birds are the only nocturnal fruit-eating birds on earth.

40. The most common non-wild bird in the world is the chicken.

41. Flamingos often pair for a lifetime and some stay with their mates for 40 years or more.

42. Some scientists believe that birds evolved from dinosaurs during the Mesozoic Era.

43. The Emperor Penguin is the only bird that lays its eggs in the middle of winter.

44. There are over 40 million pet birds in the United States of America.

45. The toes of an ostrich are shaped like that of an antelope.

46. The type of food that a bird eats in the wild is determined by the shape of a bird's beak.

47. The eyes of an ostrich are bigger than any other land animals' eyes and are even larger than their brain.

133

48. The larger a bird, the more likely it is to survive and live longer in the wild.

49. The reason why birds don't fall off of a branch when they sleep is that their toes automatically clench around the twig they are standing on.

50. A European wren's song has about 700 distinct notes per minute.

Image of European wren

51. The male ostrich can willingly take care of other females' eggs and is the only bird that does so.

52. A Ruby-throated Hummingbird has to beat its wings more than 50 times a second to hover in front of a flower.

53. The Emperor Penguins are able to stay underwater for up to 18 minutes.

54. The bird with the longest wingspan is the Wandering Albatross.

55. Arctic terns have the longest annual migration of any bird and can cover up to 25,000 miles (40233.6 km) in migration.

56. Crows are able to share their grudge against a specific person with other crows.

Image of Crows

57. The largest and tallest bird in the world is the ostrich, their males can reach up to 8 feet.

58. Hummingbirds are the only birds that are able to register negative speeds.

59. The highest-flying bird in the whole world is the Griffon Vulture.

60. The smallest bird that immigrated is the Rufous hummingbird.

61. The biggest bird that ever existed is the flightless elephant bird although it is now extinct.

62. Oil birds eat a lot of oil palm fruits and this makes the birds oily too.

63. Hummingbirds are the species of birds that build the smallest nests among other birds.

64. The Peregrine Falcon is the fastest flying bird in a dive with speeds up to 110 mph (177kph).

Image of a Peregrine Falcon

65. Birds are able to sense small changes in air pressure, which is important in predicting weather changes.

66. Swifts also spend most of their lives in the air and can even sleep in the air.

67. The Sooty Tern spends more time in the air than any other bird in the world.

68. Birds typically have up to 3 fingers on each of their wings.

69. Birds are the only vertebrates that have a fused collarbone.

70. A group of owls has interesting names which are, parliament, study, or wisdom.

71. The Bald Eagle builds the largest tree nest of all birds and it can measure up to 9.5 ft across.

72. While immigrating, the linear formation of the birds is mostly "V" or "L" shape.

73. An albatross can soar for as long as five straight hours without moving its wings.

Image of an Albatross

74. The heaviest bird in the air is the Kori Bustard which weighs about 31 lb.

75. The fastest level flight by a bird has been seen in both Red-breasted Merganser and Spine-tailed Swift.

76. The stomach acid of a vulture is 10 to 100 times stronger than human stomach acid

77. The bird that moves the slowest while flying is the American Woodcock.

78. A group of crows have a weird collective name and are called a murder or congress.

79. Falcons and kestrels have about the same power of sight as human beings.

80. Lighthouses are dangerous for birds because many are killed when they fly into the glass.

81. Birds know winter is coming when there are changes in hormones that cause them to put on fat.

82. Crows have an unusual ability to recognize and remember human faces.

83. Woodcocks and many ducks have a 360-degree field of vision because of the placement of their eyes.

Image of a Woodcock

84. The most dangerous among all birds in the world is the Cassowary.

85. A woodpecker's tongue can be up to 4 inches (10.16cm) long depending on the species.

86. The earliest known bird is the Archaeopteryx which lived during the Jurassic period.

87. The stomach acid of a vulture is so corrosive that it can digest carcasses infected with anthrax.

88. There are some birds that have feathers that are waterproof and UV rays resistant.

89. Eleven percent of bird species in the world are endangered.

90. Bats are the only mammals that are able to fly like birds.

91. Since 1600, more than one hundred and fifty kinds of birds have become extinct.

92. Among all the Eagle species, only the Wedge-tailed Eagle can see better than humans.

93. Ruppell's Vulture can reach an altitude of 11,277 meters high while flying.

94. Birds generally have a lowered sense of taste compared to other animals.

95. Birds are completely unable to sweat and need to breathe most of the time to keep cool.

96. The body temperature of birds is 7 to 8 degrees hotter than humans.

97. Only about 20% of bird species migrate long distances every year.

98. Pelicans can hold up to 11 kilograms of fish and water in their beak.

Image of a Pelicans

99. The egg of an ostrich needs about 2 hours for it to be hard-boiled.

100. Only about 25 percent of wild birds survive past the age of six months.

101. Wren can bring up to 500 caterpillars and spiders to its nestlings during a single afternoon forage.

102. The Honey Bird can lead humans to a beehive in exchange for some honey.

103. Birds do not have the best life expectancy as most of them do not live more than a decade.

104. The larger a bird, the more it is likely to live longer in the wild.

105. Eagles are so strong that they can fly away with a young deer in their claws.

Image of an Eagle

Peacock Facts

1. The name Peacock refers only to the male folks of the peafowl family.

2. There are three species of peafowl, one species from Africa and the other two from Asia.

3. In the wild, a peafowl can live up to 25 years, and in captivity, up to 50 years.

4. Make pea fowls are about twice the size of the female pea fowls.

5. Peacocks are impressive runners and have an average speed of 10 miles per hour (16km/h).

6. The colorful tail that male pea fowls have is known as a train.

7. Peacocks are known to fly once in a while when it is running away from predators.

8. Peacocks are not solitary animals and love to live in groups known as harems.

9. The Congo peafowl is the only species of peafowl that have been listed as vulnerable.

10. Peacocks have been kept in human captivity for more than 2000 years.

11. During breeding seasons, peahens can lay as many as six eggs.

12. Peacocks' meals consist of plants, insects, and certain reptiles and amphibians.

13. Male peafowl has a minimum of two partners in the wild and as many as five.

14. The peacock is one of the largest flying birds on earth with a wingspan of 4.9 feet.

15. During the time Peacocks are born, they do not have tails.

16. Male peafowl replenishes their feathers every year for them to look more colorful.

Eagle Facts

1. The eyesight of an Eagle is 4 times better than that of a human being.

2. There are so many species of eagles, which are up to sixty in number.

3. Because of the good eyesight it has, eagles are able to see about 3 kilometers away.

4. The diet of an Eagle includes fish, small mammals such as rodents, bats, and even reptiles such as snakes.

5. The lifespan of the average Eagle is about twenty years.

6. The oldest wild eagle known to exist lived for up to 38 years.

7. When eagles are living in captivity, they can live up to 50 to 70 years.

8. The age of an Eagle determines how bent its beak will be.

9. The Bald Eagle is a species of eagle that was chosen as a national symbol of the United States.

10. The more the beak of an Eagle bends, the more it becomes hard for them to feed.

11. Eagles fly so high that they can fly as high as 15,000 feet.

12. When eagles are flying they don't use much energy as they glide most of the time.

13. Eagles are one of the fastest birds on the planet and can fly as fast as 160 kilometers per hour.

14. Baby eagles reach full growth at 12 weeks old and this is when they take their first flight.

15. Unlike what people think, mother eagles do not push eagles to fly, rather they delay their food and allow them to fend for themselves.

16. It is forbidden to track or do anything malicious to eagles in the United States.

17. Eagles know how to balance their feathers so that they can glide very well in the air.

18. Male and female eagles are known to be couples throughout their lifetime.

Owl Facts

1. There are many species of owls in the world, about 200 species.

2. Owls are found everywhere in the world except Antarctica.

3. Owls are known to have binocular vision, which is the same vision human beings have.

4. Owls are primarily nocturnal birds of prey that fit in one of two families which include the barn owl and other types of owls.

5. Several owl species have ear tufts on their heads that are not real ears.

6. A parliament, wisdom, bazaar, or study is regarded as a group of owls.

7. Not all owl species are nocturnal as some of them are active during the day.

8. Females are larger, heavier, and more aggressive than male folks.

9. Owls have specialized feathers with fringes of varying softness which makes it possible for them to be silent while flying.

10. A barn owl can eat a lot of mice each and up to 1,000 mice annually.

11. Owls are carnivorous and will eat rodents, mammals, insects, fish, and other birds.

12. Owls are known to eat smaller owls of the same species.

13. An owl has three eyelids one is used for blinking, one for sleeping, and one for keeping the eye clean.

14. Owls have superior hearing and the ability to pinpoint where the prey is, even if they can't see it.

15. Owls can hear noises ten times more than human beings can hear.

16. Owls are able to rotate their eyes to about two hundred and seventy degrees.

17. Owls are known to have zygodactyl feet with two toes pointing forward and two toes pointing backward.

Chicken Facts

1. Chickens are the closest living relative to the T. rex, a species of dinosaur.

2. Studies show that chickens survive a predator attack 90% of the time in the wild.

3. Being packed in a small space causes stress which leads to feather-pecking and cannibalism.

4. Chickens in the wild lay only approximately 10 to 15 eggs annually during the breeding season.

5. Chickens dream just like human beings and they experience REM (rapid eye movement).

6. Chickens show some form of mathematical reasoning, self-control, and even structural engineering.

7. Chickens have pain receptors, enabling them to feel pain and distress just like human beings.

8. Chickens communicate with more than twenty vocalizations.

9. Chickens have a full-color vision, just like the way human beings have.

10. Chickens can identify between more than 100 different species' faces.

11. More chickens are raised and killed for food than all other land animals combined.

12. Chickens eat grass the way human beings eat spaghetti.

13. Research from scientist's shows that chickens are more brilliant than toddlers.

14. Chickens know who the eldest in the group is.

15. Mother hens are known to talk to their unborn babies.

16. Chickens are known to follow the part of the sun and Earth's magnetic field.

17. Unlike humans that are taught to count, chickens are born with the capacity to count up to five.

Ostrich Facts

1. Ostriches are the largest and heaviest living bird on the earth.

2. The Ostrich is a species of bird that is native to Africa.

3. Ostriches prefer to live in hot and dry climatic conditions.

4. According to scientists, Ostriches have existed for the past 70 to 120 million years.

5. The population of ostriches is estimated to be around two million.

6. Ostriches can be found in almost every part of the world except Antarctica.

7. Ostriches are omnivorous birds, so they eat both plants and small animals.

8. An average ostrich weighs between 150 to 330 pounds (68kg to 149.7kg).

9. Ostriches can survive without water for long periods of time.

10. Ostrich often swallows pebbles and sand that help them in grinding up their food.

11. Ostriches don't drink water often as it obtains an adequate amount of water from the plants they eat.

12. Male ostriches are about 6 to 9 feet tall while females are about 5.5 to 6.5 feet tall.

13. The normal body temperature of an ostrich is between 103 and 104 Fahrenheit.

14. Male ostriches tend to be black and white in color while females are gray.

15. Ostrich has the biggest eyes in the entire animal kingdom and they are often 2 inches (5.08cm) in diameter.

16. Ostriches are fast runners and can run up to 50 miles per hour (80.4km).

17. Male and female ostriches take turns looking after their eggs.

Dove Facts

1. Doves can be found everywhere in the world with the exception of the Sahara desert and Antarctica.

2. Female doves will usually have one or two eggs in each breeding season.

3. Dove chicks are dependent on their parents and are fed by them.

4. Some doves mate for life, while others mate only for the mating season depending on the species.

5. Research shows that doves can use landmarks as signposts while traveling.

6. Doves are excellent navigators and make use of the sun and Earth's magnetic field while flying.

7. Desert dove species get their water from plants because of the lack of water in the desert.

8. Doves drink a lot of water because they need to digest the seed they eat.

9. The major constituent of the dove's diet is seeds and fruits depending on the species.

10. Doves can be migratory while some are sedentary depending on the species.

11. The average dove weighs from 22 grams to above 2,000 grams.

12. Within groups of doves, there are dominant hierarchies among them.

13. Doves can be either solitary or very social depending on the species.

14. Doves are known to be stout-bodied with short necks and short beaks.

15. Doves are some of the strongest fliers in the world because of their strong wing muscles.

16. Doves are known to have 11 primary feathers and low wing loadings.

17. The height of doves can range from 15 centimeters to 75 centimeters.

18. Doves are known to live between 10 to 12 years depending on the species.

Duck Facts

1. Ducks can be found in every part of the world except Antarctica.

2. The egg of a duck is so heavy that it can weigh more than the hen.

3. Ducks are impressive divers and can dive up to 240 feet into the water.

4. Ducks can fly very fast and can achieve an airspeed of 100 miles per hour (160.9km/h).

5. According to research, ducks that hatch earlier tend to survive longer.

6. Ducks can have as many as 12,000 separate muscles to control their feathers.

7. More than 11% of female ducks may produce two broods each breeding season.

8. Ducks are good at flying and are capable of reaching heights of 21,000 feet.

9. A duck's beak varies by species and is classified into flat and pointed bills.

10. According to research, ducks may show a preference for colors such as blue and green.

11. Duckbills are sensitive and they are unique just like human fingerprints.

12. Ducks can sleep with one eye open in order to look out for predators that may attack as they sleep.

13. Ducks have the ability to move each of their eyes independently.

14. Ducklings have been observed to understand the relationship between objects.

15. Ducks have exceptional visuals and can see better than human beings.

16. Ducks have the ability to store information on the opposite sides of their brain.

17. Ducks in the city are typically louder than those in the forest.

Geese Facts

1. Geese are known to like the intake of fertilized grass in their food rather than unfertilized ones.

2. Baby geese can walk around and swim for a day or two days after hatching.

3. Males are called ganders, females are called geese, and babies are called goslings.

4. Migratory geese will fly up to 3,000 miles (4828km) while migrating to their birthplace.

5. Domestic geese can reach up to 10kg in weight and this is why they hardly fly.

6. A group of geese on the ground is a gaggle and when they are flying, they're called a skein.

7. It takes about 2 years for baby geese to be fully mature and start a family.

8. The egg of geese can weigh up to 120-170g depending on the species.

9. Wild geese will lay up to 5-12 eggs per year while domesticated ones can lay up to 50 eggs.

10. When goslings hatch, their parents introduce them to open water within 24 hours.

11. Domesticated geese are not monogamous and have multiple partners.

12. Wild geese usually fly in a "V" formation to help other geese that are finding it difficult to fly.

13. Geese are known to occasionally honk to encourage those in front of them to maintain speed whenever they are flying.

14. Wild geese are monogamous and have one partner throughout their lifetime.

15. Geese are preferred by farmers because they require less attention than any other farm bird.

16. Geese can be used for security because of the loud noise they make when they sight predators or strangers.

17. Geese help and protect other geese that are in trouble such as when they fall out of a tree.

Hawk Facts

1. There are about 270 species of Hawks in the world and 25 species in the United States.

2. The most common hawk in North America is the red-tailed hawk.

3. All the known species of hawks hunt their prey from the air as they fly.

4. The largest species of hawk in the world is the Ferruginous Hawk.

5. The smallest species of hawk that is found in North America is the sparrow hawk.

6. Species of hawks can be found in every part of the world with the exception of Antarctica.

7. The diet composition of hawks includes small mammals, snakes, fish, birds, and amphibians.

8. The hawk is very important in the food chain because they help control populations of smaller rodents and other animals.

9. The lifespan of hawks in the wild ranges from ten years to thirty years in the wild.

10. Red-tailed Hawks eat a lot and can eat as much as 5 pounds (2.27kg) of food per day.

11. The Hawk's claws have an incredible grip force that is better than that of human beings.

12. Some species of hawks are known to have one partner for the rest of their lives.

13. Hawks prefer to stay on their own but come together during breeding seasons.

14. Hawks don't make too much noise and have only four vocalizations.

15. The claws of a hawk are so long that they can grow up to 2 inches (5.08cm).

16. Unlike other animals, the female hawk is larger than the male.

17. Hawks are known to migrate thousands of miles every year.

Turkey Facts

1. Turkeys have two stomachs which help them in the digestion of food.

2. Turkeys don't have teeth, they have fleshy spines to eat their meal.

3. Baby turkeys can fend for themselves at an early stage of life.

4. Turkeys are very fast and can reach speeds of 25 miles per hour (40km/h).

5. Turkeys are very intelligent and can visualize a map of their territory.

6. Turkeys can recognize each other by sound and patterns.

7. Turkey's snood changes color according to the turkey's physical and mental health.

8. Turkeys sleep in trees to prevent predators from eating them.

9. Turkey poop tells a lot about them, poops that are "J" shaped are from the males while those that are spiral-shaped are from the females.

10. Turkeys, just like most farm birds, are not solitary animals, they live in groups.

11. Turkey meat contains the amino acid tryptophan and it has a calming effect.

12. Turkeys can fly but only for short distances such as a hundred yards.

13. The North American wild turkey population was almost wiped out in the 20th century but has been revived.

14. Turkeys are not water animals but they can swim if they mistakenly get inside water.

15. The dangly appendage that hangs from the turkey's forehead to the beak is called a snood.

100 Random Trivia Questions for Kids

1. What is the total number of colors in a rainbow?

2. What is used to measure temperature?

3. What animal is the fastest on land?

4. The largest of the big cat family is?

5. A spider has how many legs?

6. Which is the biggest animal on earth?

7. What is the only Substance on earth you can use to cut a diamond?

8. A baby goat is called what?

9. Name the largest planet in our solar system?

10. The zoo is a place to see what?

11. What is the number of wheels on a tricycle?

12. Which part of the body do you use in seeing?

13. How many seconds are in a minute?

14. The smallest planet in our solar system is?

15. What is the name of the smallest dog breed?

16. Which animal is the heaviest land mammal?

17. What city was the birthplace of the Olympic Games?

18. What do you get when you boil water?

19. Which color will you get when you mix blue and yellow pigment?

20. Which part of the human body pumps blood around the body?

21. How many bones do sharks have in their body?

22. How many teeth does an adult human have?

23. A group of crows called is called what?

24. What is the total number of Olympic rings?

25. The stars on the American flag are what color?

26. Which part of the body do humans use to think?

27. Which country has the highest population in the world?

28. How many players play for a team in a standard football game?

29. Which place in the world is the Eiffel Tower located?

30. Where is the statue of liberty located?

31. A group of lions is called what?

32. Name the fastest aquatic animal?

33. Where do the United States presidents live?

34. Name the smallest country in the world.

35. The largest ocean on earth is called?

36. Octopus has how many arms?

37. The Great Pyramid of Giza is located in which Country?

38. How many planets are in our solar system?

39. Name the hottest planet in the solar system.

40. What are the primary colors?

41. Which country was golf first played in?

42. Which bird has the ability to imitate human speech?

43. Which of the human body's internal organs is the largest?

44. Where does Santa Claus live?

45. How many inches make up a foot?

46. What Medal does someone who comes third in an Olympics game win?

47. How many sides does a square have?

48. What does color means stop at a traffic light?

49. Which is the largest organ in the human body?

50. A baby dog is called what?

51. Bees have how many pairs of wings?

52. Name the largest bird on earth.

53. How many bones are in the human body?

54. What is a female elephant called?

55. How big is a basketball hoop's diameter?

56. A female deer is called?

57. A million contains how many zeros?

58. An animal that can live both on the land and in the water is called?

59. What is the most common species of bird on earth called?

60. What do bees produce that humans eat?

61. How many weeks are in a year?

62. How many arms does a starfish have?

63. A group of wolves is called?

64. What is the nearest planet to the Sun in our solar system?

65. Which elements make up pure water?

66. Which country is the biggest by landmass?

67. Which planet is known to have the most gravity in our solar system?

68. How many edges does a triangle have?

69. How many days are in February in a leap year?

70. Which continent is the smallest in the world?

71. What do pandas eat mostly?

72. The longest bone in the human body is called?

73. Paper money was first used in which country?

74. The planet in our Solar System known for having a ring is called?

75. Which animal is the tallest in the world?

76. A group of sheep is called?

77. The eclipse that occurs when the Earth is between the moon and the sun is called?

78. Which is the fastest flying bird in the world?

79. What causes things that go up to fall down?

80. What is the largest continent?

81. The only flying mammal is called?

82. The process that water changes to vapor when heated is called?

83. How many stars are there on the American flag?

84. Which country gifted the Statue of Liberty to the United States?

85. A person that flies an airplane is called?

86. Who was the first man to step on the moon?

87. The tallest mountain on Earth is called?

88. A honey bee has how many eyes?

89. The preserved bones of extinct animals are called?

90. Which is the largest continent?

91. The closest star to Earth is?

92. Which direction does the Sunrise from?

93. Name the only bird that can fly backward.

94. What is the largest city in the world by population?

95. The longest river in the world is?

96. How many toes do cats have?

97. How many bones does a human newborn have when he or she is born?

98. Invertebrates are animals without which type of bone?

99. How many sides are there in Octagon?

100. The study of the Weather is called?

100 Animal Trivia Questions for Kids

1. How long can a tiger go on without feeding in the wild?

2. Newly born tiger cubs can see immediately they are born, True or False?

3. What special qualities does tiger saliva have that make them use it to clean their wounds?

4. How fast can a tiger run?

5. How long does a tiger sleep daily?

6. Tigers can stand even when they are dead, True or False?

7. What is a baby lion called?

8. Which large cat has the strongest bite?

9. At what age do lions start roaring?

10. The lion's ear is so enhanced that it can hear the sound of prey about how far?

11. Lions chew their food before swallowing, True or False?

12. The spots of a leopard are unique from others like human fingerprints, True or False?

13. How long does a leopard carry its pregnancy before giving birth?

14. How far can a Leopard jump into the air?

15. Cheetahs are able to turn mid-air when they are chasing prey, True or False?

16. What is the color of jaguar cub eyes when they are born?

17. Jaguar's cub start hearing immediately they are born, True or False?

18. How far can Cougars jump into the air?

19. The male and the female cougar are involved in taking care of their cougar cubs, True or False?

20. Can cougars roar?

21. Can cougars swim?

22. What are female tigers called?

23. Which animal has killed the most people on earth?

24. What is the most deadly snake on earth called?

25. Which animal has the shortest lifespan?

26. Can Koalas sleep up to 22 hours a day?

27. Swifts fly can fly up to six months without landing, True or False?

28. Do elephant babies suck on their trunks?

29. Which animal has the strongest bite on earth?

30. Which is the only male animal that naturally gives birth to their young ones?

31. Do pufferfish toxins have a verified antidote?

32. The land animal that has the loudest noise is?

33. Legs of an ostrich can kill a lion with a kick, True or False?

34. Which country has the highest population of pigs?

35. A baby pig is called?

36. What is the color of a white polar bear's skin?

37. How far can a great White Shark detect a drop of blood?

38. Can Naked Mole Rat survive without oxygen for 20 minutes?

39. Do piglets stand when they are born?

40. What is the most venomous fish in the world?

41. What is the biggest insect that was recorded in the world?

42. What are baby sheep called?

43. Which is the deepest fish in the ocean?

44. Which fish has both gills and lungs?

45. Can electric eels shock make a horse faint?

46. It is possible to see the organs of glass frogs, True or False?

47. Which lizard can shoot out blood from its own eye?

48. How many noses do slugs have?

49. What is the only mammal that can't jump?

50. Where do purple frogs live?

51. Which part of the body can axolotl grow back when damaged?

52. What is a baby zebra called?

53. What is the biggest land animal in the world?

54. What is the biggest snake in the world?

55. Can a Hippopotamus run faster than a human?

56. The largest land predator in the world?

57. Ostrich is native to which continent?

58. Which bird has the largest eggs in the world?

59. Which bee has the shortest lifespan in a colony?

60. Which is the only continent where you can't find frogs?

61. Can frog eat with their eyes open?

62. Can a turtle sleep underwater?

63. Turtles are warm-blooded animals, True or False?

64. Do turtles have teeth?

65. Bigger turtles and smaller turtles that live longer?

66. Can a turtle breathe underwater?

67. Can horses sleep while standing?

68. How many bones are in a horse skeleton?

69. Are baby squirrels born with their eyes open?

70. Are dog nose prints unique?

71. Australian Shepherd is an Australian dog breed, True or False?

72. How many muscles do cats have in their ear?

73. Are cats born blind?

74. Are cats born Deaf?

75. How many permanent teeth do any adult cats have?

76. What is a group of elephants called?

77. Can elephants eat meat?

78. What is a baby elephant called?

79. How many species of pandas are there on earth?

80. How many fingers do giant pandas have?

81. Are giant pandas good tree climbers?

82. What is a baby bear called?

83. A group of bears is called?

84. Are the stripe patterns on every Zebra the same?

85. Between smelly feet and clean feet, which attract Mosquitoes the most?

86. Can Sloths hold their breath underwater?

87. What is a baby fox called?

88. Can Fox pups see immediately after birth?

89. The most common species of fox in the world is?

90. Do foxes live on all continents on earth?

91. Do Kangaroos sweat?

92. Can kangaroos move backward?

93. Do penguins lay eggs?

94. Do Penguins have teeth?

95. Can Hippopotamus give birth underwater?

96. What is a group of hippopotamus called?

97. Most spiders eat their old web before starting a new one, True or False?

98. Where do rafts and spiders live?

99. Are Lizards on the continent of Antarctica?

100. What is a baby rabbit called?

50 Space Trivia Questions for Kids

1. A planet that doesn't have a defined orbital part is called?

2. How many Dwarf planets do we currently have in our solar system?

3. What is the name of the biggest dwarf planet recorded in our solar system?

4. What is the name of the dwarf planets that do not have moons?

5. Which dwarf planet is closest to the sun?

6. Which dwarf planet is closest to earth?

7. Which planet is closest to the sun?

8. Apart from Mercury, which other planet does not have a moon on its surface?

9. How many times is Jupiter bigger than the earth by mass?

10. Which planet has supersonic wind?

11. Which year was Pluto was discovered?

12. An astronaut named Charles Duke once left what in space?

13. What is the Astronaut that walked on the moon in 1972?

14. Alan Shepard was the first astronaut to play sports on the moon?

15. Do astronauts grow taller or shorter in space?

16. Why do astronauts attach themselves to something when they want to sleep in space?

17. How many moons does Neptune have as its satellites?

18. How many moons does Mars have as its satellite?

19. Which planet in our solar system has the largest number of satellites around it?

20. Do quakes occur on the moon?

21. What distance does the moon drift away from the earth yearly?

22. How many times is the mass of the sun bigger than that of the earth?

23. How long does it take the light from the sun to reach the earth?

24. The sun has enough hydrogen on its surface to burn for another how many years?

25. How many tons of oxygen does the sunburn every second?

26. How many parts is the sun made up of?

27. The type of light that the sun emits that humans can see is called?

28. At about what speed does the sun travel?

29. Helioseismology is the study of which part of the Sun?

30. Which country has launched more rockets into space than any other country in the world?

31. The force that is produced by the engine of a rocket is known as?

32. The first rocket that was launched into space in 1942 was built in which country?

33. The largest rocket on earth as of 2022 is called?

34. Light fuel rockets are more powerful than their solid-fuel rockets, true or false?

35. The most distant human-made objects from the earth are?

36. Astronomy was used to determine planting seasons in the past, true or false?

37. The first person to explain the movement of the planets was?

38. Who invented the reflecting telescope?

39. Debris in outer space is attracted to black holes because of which force?

40. The explosion of a star is?

41. The sun is heavier than the Black holes True or False?

42. Which day are asteroids celebrated yearly?

43. Which year was the first asteroid was discovered?

44. The upper atmosphere destroyed most of the asteroids that are about to hit the earth, True or false?

45. The smallest planet in the solar system is?

46. What is the closest galaxy to our milky way?

47. How long does it take the light from the sun to reach Neptune?

48. Which planet in our solar system as astronauts made more missions to?

49. The second largest planet in the solar system is?

50. Which planet has the highest mountain in the Solar System?

Answers to 100 Random Trivia Questions for Kids

1. 7

2. Thermometer

3. The cheetah.

4. Tiger

5. Eight

6. Blue Whale

7. Diamond

8. Kid

9. Jupiter

10. Animal

11. Three

12. Eye

13. 60

14. Mercury

15. The Chihuahua

16. Elephant

17. Athens, Greece

18. Steam

19. Green

20. Heart

21. 0

22. 32

23. A murder.

24. 5

25. White

26. Brain

27. China

28. 11

29. Paris, France.

30. New York

31. Pride

32. The Sailfish

33. The White House

34. Vatican City

35. The Pacific.

36. Eight.

37. Egypt

38. Eight

39. Venus

40. Red, Yellow, and Blue

41. Scotland

42. Parrot

43. The Liver

44. The North Pole

45. 12

46. Bronze

47. 4

48. Red

49. The skin

50. Puppy

51. 2

52. Ostrich

53. 206

54. A cow.

55. 18 inches

56. Doe

57. 6

58. An amphibian.

59. Chicken.

60. Honey

61. 52

62. Five

63. A pack

64. Mercury.

65. Hydrogen and oxygen.

66. Russia

67. Jupiter

68. 3

69. 29

70. Australia

71. Bamboo

72. Femur.

73. China

74. Saturn

75. Giraffe

76. Flock

77. A lunar eclipse

78. Peregrine Falcon

79. Gravity

80. Asia

81. Bat.

82. Evaporation

83. 50.

84. France

85. A pilot

86. Neil Armstrong

87. Mount Everest

88. 5

89. Fossils.

90. Asia

91. The sun

92. The east

93. A hummingbird.

94. Tokyo, Japan.

95. The Nile

96. 18

97. 300

98. Backbone

99. Eight

100. Meteorology

Answers to 100 Animal Trivia Questions for Kids

1. About 2 weeks

2. False, they are born blind.

3. Antiseptic qualities

4. 60km per hour.

5. About 18 hours

6. True

7. Cub

8. Jaguar

9. Age of 2

10. A mile away

11. False

12. True.

13. About 96 days

14. 6 meters (20 feet)

15. True

16. Blue

17. False, they are born deaf.

18. 20 feet (6.1 meters)

19. False, only the female takes care of its cubs.

20. No

21. Yes

22. Tigress

23. Mosquito

24. Inland Taipan

25. Mayfly

26. Yes

27. True

28. Yes

29. Saltwater Crocodile

30. Seahorse

31. No

32. The howler monkey

33. True

34. China

35. Piglet

36. Black

37. About 5km

38. Yes

39. No, they stand up within minutes

40. The stonefish

41. Dragonfly

42. Lamb

43. Mariana sailfish

44. Lungfish

45. Yes

46. True

47. Horned Lizard

48. 4

49. The elephant

50. Underground

51. Any part of their body

52. Foal

53. African elephant

54. Green anaconda

55. Yes

56. Polar bears

57. Africa

58. Ostrich

59. Worker bee

60. Antarctica

61. No

62. Yes

63. False, they are cold-blooded

64. No

65. Bigger turtles

66. No, but they can hold their breath

67. Yes

68. 205

69. No

70. Yes

71. False

72. 32

73. Yes

74. Yes

75. 30

76. Herd

77. No

78. Calf

79. 2

80. 6

81. Yes

82. Cub

83. A sleuth or a sloth

84. All zebra have a unique stripe pattern.

85. Smelly feet

86. Yes

87. Pups

88. They are blind until nine days after birth.

89. Red fox

90. No, live on every continent except Antarctica.

91. No

92. No

93. Yes

94. No

95. Yes

96. Herd or school

97. True

98. Water

99. No

100. Kitten

Answers to 50 Space Trivia Questions for Kids

1. Dwarf Planets

2. 5

3. Pluto.

4. Ceres

5. Ceres

6. Ceres

7. Mercury

8. Venus

9. 318 times

10. Neptune

11. 1930

12. Photos of his family

13. Gene Cernan.

14. Golf

15. Taller. They can grow about 3% taller.

16. To avoid floating around.

17. 14

18. 2

19. Jupiter

20. Yes

21. About 3.8 cm or 1.5 inches

22. About 333,000 times

23. 8 Minutes

24. 5 billion

25. About four million tonnes of oxygen.

26. 3

27. Visible light?

28. 220 kilometers per second.

29. The interior part

30. China

31. Thrust

32. Germany

33. Saturn V

34. True.

35. Voyager 1 and 2

36. True.

37. Sir Isaac Newton

38. Sir Isaac Newton

39. Gravity

40. Supernova

41. False

42. 30 June

43. 1801

44. True.

45. Mercury

46. Andromeda

47. 4 hours

48. Mars

49. Saturn

50. Mars

Tips That Will Help You Stay Safe Around Dangerous Animals.

General Safety Tips for Dangerous Animals:

1. **Stay Calm:** Never panic if you see a dangerous animal. Panicking may provoke it.

2. **Keep a Safe Distance:** Always maintain a safe distance from wild animals.

3. **Don't Approach Animals:** Even if they look calm, don't approach or touch wild animals.

4. **Don't Run:** Running might trigger a predatory response in some animals.

5. **Avoid Sudden Movements:** Sudden movements can startle animals, making them react aggressively.

6. **Stay Quiet:** Loud noises can scare animals and make them feel threatened.

7. **Do Not Feed Wild Animals:** Feeding can make animals associate humans with food and become more aggressive.

8. **Observe Wildlife from Afar:** Use binoculars to observe animals from a distance.

9. **Know Animal Habitats:** Be aware of areas where dangerous animals live and avoid them.

10. **Don't Wear Bright Colors:** Some animals, especially large cats like lions, may get attracted to bright colors.

11. **Move Slowly Around Animals:** Fast movements can be interpreted as a threat by many animals.

12. **Don't Stare Directly at Predators:** Avoid direct eye contact with animals like lions, as it can be seen as a challenge.

13. **Stay in Groups:** Animals are less likely to attack groups of people.

14. **Avoid Nocturnal Areas:** Many dangerous animals are active at night, so avoid forests or fields after dark.

15. **Learn Local Animal Signs:** Be familiar with warning signs for nearby animals, like snake tracks or bear droppings.

16. **Stay on Trails:** When hiking or in nature, stay on marked paths to avoid disturbing animals.

17. **Wear Protective Clothing:** Long sleeves and pants can protect you from animal bites and stings.

18. **Stay Aware of Surroundings:** Always be alert and listen for animal sounds when outside.

19. **Be Cautious Near Water:** Many dangerous animals, like crocodiles or hippos, live near water bodies.

20. **Learn First Aid:** Know basic first aid for animal bites or stings to respond quickly in emergencies.

Chimpanzees and Other Primates

1. **Avoid Eye Contact with Them:** Staring at a chimpanzee can be interpreted as a challenge.

2. **Do Not Feed Them:** Feeding can make them aggressive and associate humans with food.

3. **Do Not Mimic or Imitate Their Actions:** Mimicking a chimpanzee's gestures can be misunderstood as aggression.

4. **Avoid Wearing Shiny Objects:** Chimpanzees may become curious or aggressive toward jewelry or shiny objects.

5. **Move Away Slowly:** If you encounter a chimpanzee, back away slowly without turning your back on it.

6. **Stay Out of Primate Territories:** Chimpanzees can be territorial and may attack if they feel their space is being invaded.

7. **Do Not Run:** Running away from a chimpanzee could provoke it to chase you.

8. **Keep Calm if They Approach:** Remain calm and avoid any sudden movements.

9. **Don't Offer Food or Objects:** Offering objects can encourage aggressive behavior from chimpanzees.

Big Cats (Lions, Tigers, Leopards, etc.):

1. **Don't Turn Your Back on a Lion:** Slowly back away while facing the lion.

2. **Make Yourself Look Bigger:** If a big cat approaches, raise your arms to appear larger.

3. **Speak Calmly and Firmly:** Use a strong, calm voice to discourage a lion from approaching.

4. **Avoid Squatting or Bending:** Standing up straight helps reduce the likelihood of an attack from a lion.

5. **Avoid Predator Zones at Dawn and Dusk:** Lions and other big cats are more active during these times.

6. **Never Run from a Big Cat:** Running can trigger their instinct to chase.

7. **If Charged by a Lion:** Stand your ground and wave your arms, making noise to scare it off.

8. **Travel in Groups:** Lions are less likely to approach large groups of people.

9. **Avoid Eye Contact with Big Cats:** Direct eye contact can be interpreted as a threat by lions and tigers.

Snakes:

1. **Stay on Open Trails:** Avoid tall grass or dense brush where snakes may be hiding.

2. **Wear Boots and Long Pants:** Protective clothing helps reduce the risk of snake bites.

3. **Check Before Sitting or Stepping:** Always check logs, rocks, or tall grass before stepping or sitting.

4. **Don't Handle Wild Snakes:** Even small, non-venomous snakes can bite when they feel threatened.

5. **Stay Still if You See a Snake:** Most snakes won't bite unless they feel threatened. Slowly back away.

6. **Recognize Venomous Snakes:** Learn how to identify dangerous species like rattlesnakes or cobras.

7. **Avoid Reaching into Holes:** Snakes may hide in holes or crevices, so always check before reaching in.

8. **Don't Corner a Snake:** Give snakes an escape route to avoid provoking an attack.

9. **Stay Calm After a Snakebite:** If bitten, remain calm to slow the spread of venom and seek medical attention immediately.

10. **Use a Stick to Move Obstacles:** When hiking, use a stick to poke at rocks or logs to check for hidden snakes.

Bears:

1. **Avoid Surprising Bears:** Make noise when hiking to avoid startling a bear.

2. **Never Run from a Bear:** Running triggers their predatory instinct; back away slowly instead.

3. **Play Dead if a Grizzly Attacks:** Lie on your stomach, cover your head, and play dead until the bear leaves.

4. **Make Yourself Look Big:** If a bear is near, raise your arms and speak in a firm voice to make yourself appear larger.

5. **Store Food Properly:** When camping, store food in bear-proof containers to avoid attracting them.

6. **Climb a Tree Only as a Last Resort:** Black bears are excellent climbers, so don't rely on trees for safety.

7. **Use Bear Spray:** Carry bear spray when in bear territory and know how to use it effectively.

8. **Stay Away from Cubs:** A mother bear will be extremely protective of her cubs, so keep your distance.

9. **Travel in Groups:** Bears are less likely to approach groups of people.

10. **Stay Calm Around a Bear:** If a bear approaches, stay calm, speak softly, and slowly back away.

Crocodiles and Alligators:

1. **Stay Away from Water's Edge:** Crocodiles and alligators often lurk near the edges of rivers and lakes.

2. **Don't Swim in Crocodile Habitats:** Avoid swimming in areas where crocodiles are known to live.

3. **Run in a Straight Line:** If chased by an alligator, run away quickly in a straight line, not zigzag.

4. **Avoid Splashing:** Loud splashing can attract crocodiles or alligators to the area.

5. **Don't Feed Crocodiles:** Feeding encourages them to approach humans for food.

6. **Be Aware of Nesting Sites:** Female crocodiles are protective of their nests and may attack if approached.

7. **Stay in Boats:** Don't dangle limbs over the side of boats in waters known for crocodiles.

8. **Avoid Swimming at Dusk and Dawn:** These are prime feeding times for crocodiles.

9. **Observe Warning Signs:** Follow local warnings and signs that indicate crocodile or alligator presence.

10. **Leave Immediately if You See One:** Don't try to get closer for a better view or photo.

Insects (Bees, Wasps, Spiders, Mosquitoes):

1. **Avoid Bright Colors:** Bees and wasps are attracted to bright colors.

2. **Don't Swat at Bees:** Swatting may provoke them to sting. Instead, stay calm and move away.

3. **Wear Insect Repellent:** Use repellent to keep mosquitoes and ticks at bay.

4. **Stay Away from Nests:** Bees and wasps become aggressive if you come near their nests.

5. **Avoid Using Strong Perfumes:** Sweet-smelling perfumes can attract insects.

6. **Check Clothing and Skin for Ticks:** After being outdoors, always check for ticks.

7. **Shake Out Shoes and Clothes:** Insects, like spiders, can hide in clothing and shoes.

8. **Avoid Leaving Food Exposed:** Open food can attract insects like ants and wasps.

9. **Close Windows and Doors at Night:** Keep windows and doors closed to prevent insects from entering your home.

10. **Wear Long Sleeves and Pants:** Protective clothing helps prevent bites from mosquitoes, ticks, and other insects.

11. **Avoid Wearing Shiny Jewelry:** Reflective surfaces can attract bees and wasps.

12. **Eliminate Standing Water**: Mosquitoes breed in standing water, so empty containers, birdbaths, and clogged gutters.

13. **Check Shoes and Clothing**: insects often hide in shoes and clothing, so always check before wearing them.

Fishes and Sharks:

1. **Avoid Swimming at Dawn and Dusk**: Sharks are more active during these times.

2. **Don't Swim with Open Wounds:** Blood in the water can attract sharks.

3. **Stay in Groups When Swimming:** Sharks are less likely to approach groups of people.

4. **Avoid Wearing Shiny Jewelry:** Jewelry can resemble fish scales and attract sharks.

5. **Don't Splash Excessively:** Excessive splashing may attract sharks to your area.

6. **If You See a Shark, Stay Calm:** Slowly back away and get out of the water without panicking.

7. **Stay in Designated Swimming Areas:** Lifeguards often monitor these areas for shark activity.

8. **Leave the Water if Sharks Are Spotted:** Don't wait to see if they get closer; exit the water immediately.

9. **Avoid Murky Water:** Sharks may mistake you for prey in unclear waters.

10. **Know Shark Behavior:** Learn the body language of sharks, like arching their back, which can indicate aggression.

Elephants:

1. **Don't Approach Elephants:** Elephants can be unpredictable and dangerous if threatened.

2. **Stay Quiet Around Elephants:** Loud noises can startle them, causing aggressive behavior.

3. **Observe from a Distance:** Use binoculars to watch elephants from afar.

4. **Never Get Between an Elephant and Its Calf:** Elephants are protective of their young and can charge if they feel threatened.

5. **Watch for Warning Signs:** Elephants show aggression by flapping ears or trumpeting.

6. **Move Away Slowly:** If an elephant approaches, back away slowly without turning your back.

7. **Avoid Flash Photography:** Flashing lights can irritate elephants, making them aggressive.

8. **Do Not Block Their Path:** Always give elephants the right of way and avoid crowding them.

9. **Stay in Your Vehicle:** If on a safari, stay inside your vehicle when elephants are near.

10. **Know When to Run:** If an elephant charges and you have no other choice, run in a zigzag pattern to avoid being trampled.

Wolves and Wild Dogs:

1. **Don't Run from Wolves:** Running can trigger a chase response.

2. **Face the Wolf and Stand Tall:** Stand your ground and make yourself appear larger by raising your arms.

3. **Make Noise:** Yelling or clapping can scare wolves away.

4. **Don't Camp Near Wolf Dens:** Wolves are protective of their territory and may attack if threatened.

5. **Avoid Traveling Alone in Wolf Territories:** Wolves are more likely to approach someone who is alone.

6. **Carry a Walking Stick:** A walking stick can be used to defend yourself if necessary.

7. **Don't Leave Food Out:** Leaving food around attracts wolves and wild dogs to campsites.

8. **If Attacked, Fight Back:** Wolves can be deterred by aggression, so fight back if they attack.

9. **Move Slowly Away from Packs:** If you encounter a pack, slowly back away without turning your back.

10. **Stay in Vehicles or Enclosures:** When observing wolves, always stay inside a secure vehicle or enclosure.

Thank you so much for purchasing this book and making it this far in the book!

I greatly appreciate the time your kid took to read the facts and answer the trivia questions in this book.

As a small publisher, knowing that this book is both fun and educational to your kid, means a lot to me.

If you have 60 seconds, hearing your honest feedback on Amazon about what your kid thinks of this book, would mean the world to me.

It does wonders for the book, I love hearing about your kid's experience with the book.

How to leave a feedback:

- Open your camera app or QR code Scanner.

- Point your mobile device at the QR code below

- The review page will appear in your web browser.

OR Visit: funsided.com/FAK

Made in the USA
Columbia, SC
11 December 2024

49077770R00113